Pinwill's book immediately challenges our system of economic rewards and centralised control. It is excessively plausible, and this is reinforced throughout. A most commanding critique of how the elites use financial techniques to control the human organism, *Where Money Comes From* offers better ways in the service of true human satisfaction.

This book will knock the world sideways into common sense.

Where Money Comes From

The Explosive Truth

Charles Pinwill

LOGOS

Book Cover by Red Box Studios, redboxstudios.com.au

First edition April 2023

CONTENTS

To the Warriors who have taken care
In choosing their enemies wisely,
And taken their training from where it is best had
Rather than most persistently advocated.

Part One

WHERE ARE THESE ESSAYS TAKING US?

Explaining DMC

D emocratic Money Creation (DMC) is a proposal to change the way in which money is created, owned, and distributed.

Over 95% of modern money is now in the form of bank deposits. Less than 5% is in the form of notes or coins made by the mint.

The 95% is created by our banking system. This is done by banks making loans which, when spent, become someone's bank deposit. Since no one's deposit is ever reduced to make a loan, the amount of deposits is increased by the amount of new loans.

When deposits are used to repay loans, this cancels out deposits, and reduces the money in existence.

This system has several consequences:

1. At the point of creation, all money is the property of the banking system.

2. Since all new money is created as loans, all of society's money is owed to the banks as debt. The community has no money at all in *net terms*.

3. Since the cost of consumer production includes the incomes paid to us to produce consumables, plus capital costs and overheads, our incomes alone cannot buy it all. If all consumer products are to be sold, the

money supply must be regularly increased to enable this. All countries must increase the money (debt) in existence each year by at least 10%, and they do.

4. This results in burgeoning debt. In trillions, America's debt is $90, and the world's is $200.

5. Costs and prices must forever increase to service this increased debt. Inflation is the consequence, as is widespread financial hardship.

Because banking elites have the power to costlessly create our money and own it, their influence over the media, education and public policy in all areas is enormous, and usually decisive. If political democracy struggles against this, it is usually ineffectual.

So, what does DMC suggest?

1. That a National Credit Authority be established with court-like powers to determine the amount of any needed money supply increase. This would be done by measuring the national economy with National Profit and Loss Accounts and Balance Sheets, in the same way that companies do these accounts.

2. This NCA would be empowered to create money to the extent that a deficiency of consumer purchasing power exists, and to distribute this money as a national dividend on the basis that all people would receive an equal share.

3. Banks would continue to finance production in the normal way, but would no longer be permitted to finance consumption, as this would be done through the National Dividend.

This would mean that:

1. The National debt would no longer increase every year. Indeed, the

national dividend's debt free funds would be available to progressively pay it down.

2. Debt charges in prices and taxes would atrophy thus reducing costs and prices.

3. Mortgage and debt repayments would no longer dominate our lives and public policy.

4. In receiving "money votes" on the same basis that ballot papers are distributed, we would add economic democracy to political democracy.

5. The mega-funding for the *Great Reset* would be disabled.

The increase in personal sovereignty which DMC offers, while beyond the reach of so short an explanation, would bring cultural, social, economic, and political benefits which, while perhaps dimly perceived at present, will progressively be available to ourselves and future generations.

PROLETARIATS OR PROPRIETORS?

T he role of socialism these last two hundred years has been to represent the proletariat. There is nothing wrong with representing the proletariat. Socialists of all types, Trade Unionists, Fabians, Communists and Social Democrats have all seen this as their special role in political and economic life. Their motive has largely been one of compassion in helping the economically disenfranchised; a commendable aspiration.

It has unfortunately usually brought the conceptual limitation of seeing the proletarian status of most people as being in the main, an unavoidable and eternal condition with little prospect of amendment. This has not been wholly so, for many have championed such as home ownership and superannuation for the working public.

However, those who have represented the builders, butchers and bakers (notwithstanding the provision of social security in dire need) have ever seen the wage as the sole means of sustenance for most. But the world is changing, and we are going to have to look a little further in the coming technological revolution.

Technology is both displacing employment and making it both more productive and efficient. Those who see that this is threatening unemployment are missing a major and world changing consideration. Industrialised societies are becoming more profitable in a hitherto little observed way, and this has now been measured and demonstrated.[1]

In the United States in 2014 the total aggregated income of all US citizens amounted to $10.1 trillion. This was the amount paid to Americans to induce them to produce the sum total of consumer products of $12.5 trillion which were both produced and sold. The excess in value of consumer products over consumes' incomes given above, was a total deficiency of consumer incomes of $2.4 trillion. This is surely a societal profit!

This profit of $2.4 trillion amounted to $7,500 per person over the whole population, or to $30,000 per family of four.

Modern democracies practice universal suffrage (we all get one vote), and this is in recognition of the fact that we all have a share in the ownership of our respective countries.

If this is allowed, might we also have a just claim to a part of the societal profit?

Americans only got access to this societal profit in 2014 by increasing their total indebtedness to their banking system by $2.3 trillion. It doesn't have to be done this way. Modern money is almost wholly in the form of digital IOUs created in cyberspace.

These IOUs (US dollars) are issued as claims upon the Nation's assets and products. They are liabilities which would be issued against the National Balance Sheet if nations did normal accounts. The aforementioned accounts are essential if we are ever to realise the prospect of our proletariat, even those with no investment capital, becoming, and increasingly becoming proprietors sharing in the societal profit issued to them as a National Dividend.

The mechanics of doing this would require the establishment of something in the nature of a National Credit Authority, appropriately empowered to calculate the national profit from our increasing technology, and to issue credit

---

1. See the Prototype National Accounts posted in the Advanced Library at: http://www.socialcredit.com.au/uploads/NationalAccountsPrototype.pdf

against our National Balance Sheet and distribute it in the form of a National Dividend payable to all.

The banking system would need to be constrained from issuing consumer credit to a like amount. Though politically difficult, especially in our current state of national accounts which are wholly inadequate when viewed from the standpoint of common best practice by all corporations, it has social implications of the utmost importance.

With the increasing displacement of human labour from the economy, and an ever-expanding debilitating debt in all sectors of society, the logic is inescapable and the ultimate unavoidability of having all share in a national dividend to maintain the functionality of the economy, summonses the spectre of inevitability.

Not the spectre envisioned by Karl Marx of us all becoming proletariats, but rather of all becoming progressively, and increasingly, proprietors.

PART TWO

ESSAYS WHICH MAY HELP IN UNDERSTANDING, AND PERHAPS ONE DAY ACHIEVING, DEMOCRATIC MONEY CREATION

A CAVALRY OF ACCOUNTANTS

This essay's title is not suggesting a collective term whereby an assembly of numerous accountants might be known. The expressions a gang of thieves, a murder of crows, a parliament of baboons or a melancholia of economists are expressions giving an indication of what might normally be expected from them given the nature of these beings.

One would not, in everyday experience, expect to see mounted accountants waving their abaci and electronic calculators and brandishing their books of account, as they rode fearlessly to confront the enemies of sound statistical data. But this is very much needed as we shall see.

Accountants spend most of their working lives associating with people who like facts, like knowing what is going on, and who want things to be measured and understood. Directors of companies large and small, and even such as the treasurer of the local tennis club, like to know something of what they are doing. They ask their accountants to tell them whether they are making a profit or a loss, and to list their assets and liabilities.

Politicians on the other hand, only ever ask for a guess as to what may happen next year (The Budget), and a summation of the total turnover last year (The GDP).

The whole world over, company directors and association officers universally want the facts relevant to the entities they manage. Whether more value is being consumed during their productive efforts than is delivered by it, is knowledge of importance to company directors. They also have an interest in whether their assets have increased or decreased, one against the other, in any period of time.

All this is in contradistinction to the really important leadership in the world. Politicians never do or seek National Profit and Loss Accounts, or comprehensive Balance Sheets either, and economists of course, never suggest them. This is because they instinctively have and know this data subconsciously and accurately, as the brilliance with which national economies are managed makes evident.

The politicians of Canada and Australia have made some efforts to cover their embarrassment by doing limited national balance sheets a few times in the past. Neither country bothered to include their largest asset or their largest liability, so they were only pretending to want to know.

Apparently, what is spent on the vocational training of their people to produce doctors, bricklayers, engineers and bakers is completely worthless, as they didn't think to give it value as an asset in their national balance sheets. The largest claim upon a country's assets, which is what a liability is, and therefore the largest national liability, didn't rate a mention either. So therefore, many politicians to this day do not know that the money supply is a claim upon our economy, and therefore a liability.

Profit and Loss Accounts measure the value of what is produced by an entity, against the value of what is consumed and used up in that productive effort, and this from the perspective of shareholders.

The purpose of a human economy is the delivery of consumer goods. Important though the production of factories, giant oil tankers and electric power stations may be, they are only important in their assistance to the production of consumer goods. The health and profitability of a human economy can only, in the end, be measured by the value of consumer goods produced, and comparing it to the value of the recompense paid out to induce this to be done. In other words, the total consumer production compared to total personal incomes paid to do it, determines a human economy's profitability.

This was done for the first time for the USA for the year 2014 and showed that consumer production both produced and sold was $12.5 trillion, and total personal incomes were only $10.1 trillion. The profit per American was $7,500. The account which evidences this is at http://www.socialcredit.com.au/uplo ads/NationalAccountsPrototype.pdf

Because of this unacknowledged profit, the American debt had to increase by $2.3 trillion to allow the American people to augment their incomes sufficiently to consume the entire national product.

While such accounts are not done or even requested by politicians and economists, it has never occurred to them that society may be profitable; nor have any of the opportunities which may arise from national profitability ever been considered. Company directors are interested in whether their organisations are profitable and what might be done with the profit. Strangely, our parliaments of baboons and melancholia of economists exhibit no such interest.

What is needed is indeed a Cavalry of Accountants to ride into the public domain with calibrated, measured and authenticated facts about the human economy to relieve the politicians and economists of the stress of divination in managing the economy.

Perhaps we should not say "Come forth, ye brave and fierce Accountants and to a blast of trumpets and a roll of drums, triumphantly impose the needful data on our bewildered and routed economists and politicians, subject them to the gravitas of fact, run them through with statistical truth, vanquish their interminable economic muddle, cast down and subdue their monetary ignorance's folly and open up the whole world to a consideration at some remote time, and in some very timorous way, to such ideas as the teeniest tidbits of a National Dividend being paid to all in lieu of increasing the national debt"?

Never! Never will any data be tolerated, accepted or acknowledged which will enlighten us to any national profitability. The very thought of it! Indeed! What would become of us?

MONEY: A WORK IN PROGRESS

I n the beginning was one's word. And one's word was one's bond. And no transactions were ever repeated if good faith was not present in the first one. Because trust is the basis of all trading it could only initially happen within small family and tribal associations. Those who gave yet didn't receive, or received though didn't reciprocate, vetoed mutually beneficial outcomes.

This was the twinkle in the eye before the conception of money.

Barter was the beginning of it. It is generally supposed to have been particularly difficult to make desired trades. How does one find a pair of shoes in exchange for some arrowheads? A cobbler would not necessarily want the arrowheads but may accept them if he knew someone else who would want them who had suitable leather for sale. If not, then perhaps he had marmalade jam which a leather owner was known to like, or which may be exchanged for baubles which a leather owner's wife was susceptible to use.

If money was invented to make things simpler, then presumably the long chains of exchange in a barter economy must have been more complex than modern stock exchanges? Did we keep it simple, Stupid?

A universally required commodity, such as grain in ancient Egypt, simplified the intellectual exercise. Man does not live by bread alone, but without some bread he does not live at all, so everyone accepted at least some bread. A "currency" approaching universal acceptability was to be found in staple foods.

The Romans used the basic commodity salt which is evident in the English word "salary", and pecus (the Latin for "a head of cattle") from which was derived the English "pecuniary".

The key thing was that everybody wanted the commodity. Some things such as bird-of-paradise feathers in New Guinea were only of use in impressing one's neighbours, but if everyone wanted to impress their neighbours, and the neighbours were universally impressed by one's possession of these feathers, a universally acceptable currency was arrived at.

Defying later fixations, money took the forms of cowrie shells in West Africa until about 1900, porpoise and whales' teeth in Fiji, snails in the Queen Charlotte Islands, the red scalps of woodpeckers amongst Karok natives, dog's teeth on the island of San Cristobel, and sandalwood on Hawaii. The Polynesian Island of Yap used large aragonite stones ranging from about one foot to ten feet (three metres) in diameter, right up until 1939 when World War II brought different customs.

Professor Walker had defined money *"as anything, no matter of what it is made, or why people want it, which nobody will refuse to accept in exchange for their disposable goods or services."* Its only *money value* resides in the fact that other people want it. Nobody would want it at all, if it were not for the fact that all want it.

Different cultures had different money fetishes. Earlier cultures usually favoured commodity monies, as these had dual values: a practical use value, and a symbolic "claims upon others" value. Many hold that the best types of money have durability, portability, divisibility, and scarcity, but there is another desirable quality which is important too. In a famine, grain monies disappeared because people ate them. If a money was absolutely useless in the sense that it made no unique or significant contribution to sustaining life, it would not be used up in any circumstances.

The absolute uselessness of gold was a major factor in its rise as a money. Gold's irrelevance to sustaining life was closer to an absolute fact than it was with any other product, and it remains so. It is essential and irreplaceable in no useful function whatsoever. Nobody has yet nominated an element which, if all of it was removed to the other side of the moon, would do less injury to humanity than would gold. No wonder its adherents proclaim its value with such adamancy; its value is a matter of faith.

Gold was strongly supported by bankers as the basis of the issue of money for another reason. Everyone knew it was difficult to find and mine. It would therefore hold its value, was the rationale. The bankers loved it, however, for another reason: they could create and loan into society about one hundred times more money than they had gold. It is a well-known story.

When a gold sovereign was deposited, a receipt for one sovereign payable in gold was given to the depositor. As few actually wanted the gold itself - they just wanted to know that it was there - another ten receipts (bank notes) were written and loaned out. Not one in ten people wanted the gold, and when they did, they soon brought it back and redeposited it anyhow.

Next the bankers encouraged people to leave their banknotes with them too. A special account would be given them, and they could direct the bank to make payments by writing cheques. The banks now made loans by putting credit (the right to draw funds) into these accounts. For every gold sovereign, there were now ten banknotes, and for every ten banknotes there were one hundred "sovereigns" in either cheque or savings accounts.

The "scarcity" of gold was such that it could be multiplied one hundred-fold, and the community was still none the wiser. And as it turned out, this was a good thing. Why? Because the industrial revolution could now be financed, and the empire expanded to places like Canada and Australia and the industrial and economic ability of mankind exploded. This money multiplication happened everywhere of course, not just in England.

This economic boon could not have happened if the money really was gold. What most extol as a virtue of gold: its scarcity, was the problem. As Warren Buffet and others have pointed out, in the whole of human history all the gold ever mined has a limited volume. If it were all put into a classic cube of equal height, width, and length, that measurement would be 20 metres. It would easily fit onto an average suburban house block.

So, the evolution of money systems had reached, seemingly, its final form by 1900. All industrial nations had arrived at a "sound money" system, with each currency firmly based upon gold. Gold could be and was withdrawn at times, but as the value of money could only be had by spending/investing it, a frugal people receiving gold and wishing to save their money then put the gold back into their bank accounts. The system worked.

Still, senior bankers had experienced runs upon banks in the 1890s and at other times too. The English had a central bank in the Bank of England which could issue credit to private banks when in trouble, and American bankers now sought to emulate this. In 1913 the Federal Reserve Bank of America was established as the capstone of this sound money system. Then came an unrehearsed event.

When World War I commenced some people thought to play it safe. Within forty-eight hours, two percent of English depositors had withdrawn their gold. The Bank of England had no more to give. What to do?

The Government declared a two-day bank holiday and hastily printed masses of flimsy bank notes. When the banks reopened, the public was told that England was off the gold standard, and withdrawals were paid in these notes. Those who didn't like the notes were told that they could bring them back if they chose, and they would be credited to their accounts. The system carefully constructed over centuries fell down in two days.

After the war the English made an attempt to reintroduce the gold standard which was supported by Winston Churchill. By 1931 it was abandoned forever as a disaster, and he apologised.

Post-war however, the decisive arena in which the world's money system was to be decided, was America. America's industrial prowess and Americans' patriotic belief in their economy brought the "roaring twenties". A fervour of confidence had even the shoeshine boys borrowing to buy shares in American industry, and the stock market rose and rose. Not to join in was simply un-patriotic. In October 1929 the Stock Market crashed and brought the Great Depression.

America's banking fraternity then decided on a policy of returning to "sound money". Credit was restricted, but in any case, the public appetite for debt had evaporated. Poverty and hardship deepened. As debts were repaid and not re-borrowed, what people would do for a scarce dollar increased, and what dollars there were could now buy bargains everywhere.

What followed was the longest and greatest (and the last) effort to reinstate "sound money". Sound money was easily arranged; one just made it scarce. The value of the bankers' mortgages was not to be eroded by inflation. Poverty, malnutrition, and suicides would not move those who choose to improve the world with sound money. The authorities' persistence was most tenacious and held with the strongest resolve. Even in 1941 the unemployment rate in the United States was over 20% but easing credit was resisted.

The Great Depression could well have been made to last until 2029 but for one awkward and difficult man. He would not countenance credit restrictions and for all the wrong reasons. Those who favoured peace would not issue credit to finance it, but Hitler wanted war, so he had the credit issued, and Germany boomed. A perfectly good depression was thereby interrupted. The population may have been retained in a much more submissive and compliant state for many years, but for that dreadful man. Even John Kenneth Galbraith, America's leading Keynesian, stated that it was not Keynes who ended the depression, but Adolf Hitler. The Japanese helped it along of course, by bombing Pearl Harbour. Economically, happy times were here again!

After the war the "cat was out of the bag" and a depression was "out of the question". John Maynard Keynes's *General Theory* published in 1935, which presented ideas he had plagiarised and perverted from C H Douglas five years previously, was now the new economic "textbook". Credit was to be issued whether the public wanted it or not, with Government "pump-priming." A whole plethora of new household products were up for manufacture; refrigerators, washing machines, vacuum cleaners, second cars etc, so industry had much to do.

In 1920, C.H. Douglas had published his ideas that a deficiency of purchasing power was continually occurring in modern economies, and in 1923 a private meeting with New York's most prominent bankers confirmed their concurrence. They opposed his solution of credit being issued debt free and distributed to all as a National Dividend. All credit must be issued as a debt to themselves. They were not conspiring of course; they were just acting and cooperating in their own self-interest.

This recurring deficiency of purchasing power was the "missing link" in economic understanding. Every year society had to go further into debt to afford to buy its own production. Even in the Great Depression the money supply was increased every year; that it was not increased enough was the problem. Economists became obsessed with deciding whether there was a deficiency of purchasing power in the economy, and reasoning why it was so, if it was so. So many schoolboys getting to the very bottom of the theory of relativity, as it were. Whether it was so or no, could only be decided by measuring it.

This was eventually done as better statistics became available. The aggregate incomes of all Americans in 2014 was measured as $10.1 trillion. The consumer goods produced *and sold* that year amounted to $12.5 trillion.[1] The bankers created another $2.3 trillion and added it to the national debt that year, which amounted to $7,500 per American, or $30,000 per family of four. So, 20% of products did not stay on the shelves, and America did not go into severe recession.

Since it is inconceivable to most that a deficiency of purchasing power could arise in a manner of which they cannot conceive, the concept remains largely ungrasped. It must be addressed otherwise. We cannot see most radiation, gravity, or the speed of light though we believe it is there when it is measured.

If we paid our employees $10.10 to produce $12.50 worth, we would be in profit $2.40. Of course, our employees could not afford to buy the $2.40 worth, as their incomes wouldn't suffice. We could, however, allow them to go into debt to us for the $2.40, and add an amount like this to the national debt each year. Their indebtedness would grow inexorably and interminably

---

1. National Accounts at http://www.socialcredit.com.au/uploads/Nationa
   lAccountsPrototype.pdf

so that in time all would tug the forelock before us. In this way they, and their governments, and their intellectuals would come in time to know the meaning of life.

Credit rules, OK.

As technology displaced human labour, improved methods and practices increased productivity, and processes were increasingly automated, the nations became more and more profitable. This being so, a larger and larger percentage of consumer products could not be purchased except by increasing indebtedness. Societies' continuance depended upon it. But how to do it?

The key was in financing housing. The banks, by lending larger sums to more people to bid against each other, could expand loans for residential dwellings, seemingly forever. If they loaned $500,000 to six different families to buy a house at auction, how much would it bring? Later if they loaned $800,000 to six families to buy it, would it now fetch $800,000? In time, two-thirds of all the money in existence had originally come into existence by the banks creating credit to fund housing.

There was so much money in the economy from housing loans by the year 2000, that industry now borrowed less as it could raise capital from trading profits or selling equity. Increasing house prices by increasing housing loans was now, overwhelmingly, the one way of keeping the economy out of recession. And as nations' profitability increased each year, so housing finance was likewise increased to keep the system "liquid". This needed to be done at an increasing rate, so credit was issued less stringently.

People without income or even prospects of income could now borrow. Their mortgages would be bundled with others and on-sold. Debt roared into the economy. In Australia the amount of money in existence increased by 19% in 2007.

Defaulting mortgages, quietly breeding in the dark, now burst forth in profusion; the Global Financial Crisis of 2008 had arrived.

Notwithstanding this inconvenience, the money supply must still be expanded or an horrific depression would occur and social unrest might take us anywhere. But nobody would borrow to buy housing just now, as the unthinkable had now been thought. How can we possibly increase debt to keep the economy going?

Having benefited from C. H. Douglas's insights, another stage was reached in this work in progress. Interest rates were reduced, sometimes to negative rates, and billions in money supply increases were rushed into the marketplace. A productive purpose was not thought necessary, but the business was in need of a name. The baby was hastily christened *Quantitative Easing* and the silver spoon pressed to his mouth to the extent of $80 billion per month. The debt economy was resuscitated yet again.

Once again, the admission that the nation's economy was profitable was avoided, and the shareholders who own this profit (We the People) had their dividend stolen and loaned to some worthies who would render an interest payment to the bankers in due season, albeit sadly at a reduced interest rate.

Thus, another step towards an inevitable outcome was taken. Universal adult suffrage is now in situ as the norm in politics; to each go an equal number of votes which don't attract interest, and the ballot papers are not repayable either. The system presumes that the voting public owns the country.

One day we may presume that We the People each own a share in the economic enterprises we call nations also.

The changes from even a century ago are profound. No longer is keeping money scarce attempted; none are brave enough to impose recession. Interest rates have also been discontinued except for nominal ones, as the public disinclination to accept more debt dictates this. The one remaining relic from the past is that loans are required to be repaid. Can this requirement also be abandoned?

The conditions of the economy are conspiring to make it so. The electric car manufacturer, Tesla, has been working at producing driverless vehicles. They report that this has involved doing so much in advancing automation and robotisation, that probably most current human employment will become redundant once these technologies are applied. The unemployed and unemployable will lose the luxury of being creditworthy, and the poor dears will be unable to be encumbered with debt. Will these vast numbers of unemployed (and therefore unem**pay**ed) consent to starving to death?

If debt is to be insisted upon, then on whom will this luxury be bestowed? Presumably the only remaining taxpayers - that is, those continuing in employment, with Government sometimes acting as an intermediary which will accept the debt and then pass it to those with continuing income. By this time wages, which will have to be high enough to allow these taxes to be paid and allow a life supporting residue for the worker, will be higher. This will add to the incentive to displace them with more technology.

How far can it be to "preposterousnessity"? Can half the employable pay all society's costs? If only 10% are required to work, shall their recompense be ten times the average living cost? At some point the insistence that income must only be funded as debt will become unhinged. Life itself decrees this, not dogma.

Dollars, like any mathematical numbers, can be created with either negative or positive signs before them (-$1.00 or +$1.00). The choice is between a National Debt or a National Dividend. Many will insist that a National Dividend is "something-for-nothing" and being true to their convictions, will determine to expire of malnutrition rather than suffer its indignity. That will leave the rest of us.

Perhaps Darwin was right, and it will, after all, be decided upon survival of the fittest.

SLAVERY, WORK AND SERVICE; THE THREE AGES OF MAN?

BY EDWARD MINTON

T he words "Slavery, Work and Service" describe a tripolar though singular world; something considered an impossibility in physics, though a commonality in metaphysics. While worlds apart, they share the same substance, as it were.

Each of these three is readily interchanged with the others when its connotations are judged to serve an effect. A mother willingly serving her family in the kitchen, when it suits, will be described as "Slaving over a hot stove" or "Working her fingers to the bone". A bureaucrat whose only motive is his salary, and only delight in his work is in casting every available stumbling block in front of any public he contacts, is described as a "Public Servant". A retiree who serves charity without recompense, is proclaimed to be "Working for charity."

Whether poetry or prose, literary license has its value, though when precise semantics are needed, one would wish it away. For the purposes of this essay we need clear differentiation to make the case. So firstly, what is the common property or essential attribute of these words which runs them together in our minds? Surely the answer is *service.*

In the first, "*slavery*", service is compelled, the choice of withholding it made in the face of punishment or death. In the second, "*work*", service is given in exchange for some recompense, while "*service*" itself is purely an act of giving to another. Its object is seen in its benefit to the receiver, though it is always accompanied in the benefactor by the joys associated with giving.

Our differentiation of meaning compares with the distinctions between rape, prostitution and love making. Is the sexual act compelled, traded, or freely given? Seen in this way, the often-made claim for "the dignity of labour", depends upon whether one is comparing the prostitutional status of work to rape, or to love making. That the connotations of "work" and "prostitution" should be equated, is outrageous at the beginning of the 21st century. At the 31st century, after a thousand years of applying the silicon chip and advancing processes, will serving for anything other than love be considered with distaste and abhorrence?

Oh dear, I have kicked over a bucket of worms! What is a "bludger", as he sits quietly watching automated processes deliver humanity's every material need, and whose intervention into production with work would only endanger its delivery of abundance? If his life is lived wholly in self-centred taking, he remains a bludger, I suppose. However, if he is busy teaching his grandchildren to play a musical instrument, visiting the sick, helping a charity, coaching a boys' sporting team, or some such, he is then a member of the ***Aristocracy of Service***, though he may never have done a day's work in his life.

This is not so futuristic, as historically speaking, the 4th millennium will gallop up with all the speed with which next Christmas arrives for old men. We are already living (arguably) in something like the 11th millennium since farming first established civilization.

During all the years which we now describe as being "B.C.", though there are at least half a million documents in the cuneiform of Mesopotamia, plus Egyptian hieroglyphics, classical Greek and Latin, Hebrew, and Phoenician etc. there is not a single statement of conscience in opposition to the institution of chattel slavery. Aristotle thought that some had been enslaved unjustly, though he always accepted the legitimacy of the institution itself. In ancient Rome up to 80% of the population were slaves by some accounts, and the Greek tribes, conquering what we now know as Greece, are thought to have subdued and enslaved a populace ten times their own number.

The Golden Age of Greece is a monument to the efficacy of slavery. They didn't have even a word for work, but spoke only in terms of what we would translate as negotiation. Their word "ergon" meant "action" or "deed" as much as it might mean "work". Their word "diploma" we have adopted to mean forming relationships by way of negotiation.

In the true age of slavery there was no work; only slavery properly so called, and then all the rest of man's economic arrangements were but negotiation, arrangement, organisation and the like. There were, in the sense in which we use the words here, pretty much no workers, just slaves and negotiators.

The first beginning of the passing of the age of slavery came gently, quietly, and almost innocuously. It started with a brief letter written by St. Paul to his friend Philemon, who had sent him a slave, one O-nes-i-mus, "...who might have ministered unto me...". This Christian slave was returned by Paul "Not now as a servant, but above a servant, a brother beloved...". The Church came to the view, beginning here, that those perceived to have been redeemed by Christ in the shedding of His blood, ought not to be re-enslaved by their fellow men. The torpedo into the Age of Slavery was off and running, and fully arrived only about 1,800 years later at approximately the time of Wilberforce. From here on, and for the foreseeable future, men would live out their lives in the Age of Work.

In the centuries in which scarcity was ever present in the human economy, St. Paul decreed that "He who will not work, neither shall he eat". If the ship is badly holed, it's "all hands to the pumps". If survival is a hard-fought struggle, it is but fair that all should contribute.

Work, after all, is not an end, but a means. A better means of pumping water than using human or animal muscles was contributed by James Watt in his steam engine, which led on to the railways. The discovery of petroleum and the internal combustion engine gave us the tractor and personal transport. The silicon chip is eliminating men from repetitive processes.

While farm production steadily rose, the percentage of the workforce employed in farming fell in the U.S.A. and Australia from 40% in 1900, to 1 or 2% in 2013, by which time obesity had displaced want and undernourishment as the chief concern with food.[1] The word-processor reduced document production by more than 90%. The attrition of employment in manufacture is advancing everywhere. In countries with low wages, the fort is being held, but the robots are at the gates. Robots manufactured by robot-manufacturing robots - which work at a much faster rate, and three times longer each day, without offsite accommodation, food (other than electricity), or thought of industrial relations, medical attention, aged care or entertainment - are infiltrating and sabotaging the standing armies of workers everywhere.

It has all long ago reached the point of tragicomedy. Every business is striving might and main to reduce labour input, and another group of people are sustaining a counter-effort to "achieve full employment". Both camps generally regard the efforts of the counter movement as worthy endeavors with desirable objects, whilst redoubling their own efforts to negate them.

So what is it which is driving this onslaught against work? In summation it is best described as our "industrial inheritance". It is no one process, technology, energy source or applied idea, but all of them and all else which has come down to us from the previous 10,000 years of achievement, learning and experience.

Why did the Greeks of classical times not work? Because they had inherited on average 10 slaves each. Why did the English nobility of Victorian times not work? Because they had inherited sufficient assets, usually in land, to make work superfluous. And why is the labour necessary for production being everywhere supplanted, notwithstanding our best efforts to retain full employment? Our whole industrial inheritance is conspiring to make life easier, and the Luddites'

---

1. The Commonwealth Yearbook, 2012, published by the Australian Bureau of Statistics, also credits Australian farmers with producing 15.8 kg of cotton lint and 17.9 kg of wool for every man, woman and child, every year. So much for the scarcity of food and clothing. It also tells us there are 7.6 million occupied private dwellings in Australia with an average of only 2.6 persons residing in each. Scarcity?

contrivances at compelling full employment are not prevailing, though through sheer tenaciousness, the inefficiency imposed upon industry by regulation and the application of fashionable verbiage in its justification, is an amazingly effective (and silly) rearguard.

The regulation of residential house building now greatly increases its cost, this leading to every compromise with quality which is possible within the regulations, the purpose of these regulations being, naturally, to ensure quality. Of course the "plus", is that making life difficult increases the employment necessary to make it easier. The charlatans who alone bring justification for these excessive regulations, usually evade due process of the law through limited liability incorporation devices. Their continuing presence in business, of course, though in small numbers, continues the propensity for full employment all the while; for wherever it is present, over-regulation acts in this manner. Still, such sandbags temporarily thrown down against the incoming tide must not be allowed to distract us.

While the motivating force behind slavery is in the whip and the sword, when, if, and as they are required, the motivation behind work is now wages paid in money, and behind inheritance is the dividend, again expressed in terms of money.

The industrial inheritance has been bequeathed to us from those who have gone before. Most of these contributors are now lost to living memory; even copyright where taken, soon lapses into the public domain. 90% of all production is now attributable to our advancing knowledge and our current tools for its application. Take the hammer, the saw, all tools and electricity, training, and knowledge away from a carpenter, and then see how long it takes him to build a house.

The transition from slavery to work came with the Act which abolished slavery in 1807. For the British this ended black slavery from Africa. Action to end white slavery in North Africa (which had taken about a million Europeans in the previous 3 centuries) came much later. In 1816 Sir Edward Pellow led 18 British men-of-war and 6 Dutch into the Port of Algiers. The ruling Dey (or Bey) Omar Bashaw, was given one hour to release his slaves and renounce slavery forever. The shore batteries of Algiers were formidable, (being built by generations of white slaves who alone in Barbary had this skill) but after several hours of the fiercest cannon fire seen at that time, they were destroyed. Next, every Algerian vessel in the port was destroyed, and the city battered and burned into the early hours of the morning until the need to rest the exhausted crews brought a calm. At dawn the Bey capitulated.[2]

The transition from a work to a service-based society is an unchartered path. We know something of the forces which drive us, and of our ultimate destination once these forces are utterly ascendant, but little about what is in the middle.

I need to say something now, with which many will find it difficult to cope. Please sit down and take a few deep breaths, and determine to suppress your wildest emotions, at least for a little while, in the hope that reflective processes will kick in. *The transition from a society of work (where one's life is surrendered for recompense), to a society of service where one's contributions to others are personally chosen and voluntarily given, is dependent upon dividends being progressively and universally distributed to all.*

While we are operating outside the bounds of "common sense", let's add insult to injury by doing an hypothetical.

Let us suppose that in many places in the world, industrial plants are established which use some futuristic nano-technology which can take any form of matter, separate it into its component atoms and molecules, and reassemble it into any and every conceivable product. These self-maintaining plants are designed to function without any attention or further energy inputs (other than solar) for 1,000 years. Their capacity exceeds all need and desire. Material security causes a loss of interest in the clutter of storing endless products against tomorrow.

If you say this is impossible, I would like to agree with you on two counts. Firstly, it is almost certainly as physically impossible as my grandfather believed man going to the moon to be. Secondly, it presents today's financial technicians

---

2. Giles Milton, White Gold, 2004, Hodder & Stoughton

with an imponderable conundrum with which they could never cope without a revolution in thought.

The investors in these plants, having spent all their money in their construction, would be anticipating a millennium of dividends. Since all labour is superfluous for the next 1,000 years, all the other people could anticipate a long pause in incomes receivable. There being no effective market for any product, since there is no income out there, there are no dividends either. The destiny of humanity is now analogous with the maggot, who starved to death because his apple was too big!

It is at this point that rocket science must come to the rescue. Money must be seen for what it is; to continue worshiping it as a supreme and inviolable entity is now clearly terminal. Money is a ticket system whose purpose is to facilitate production *and distribution*. It has no value whatever outside of its contribution towards efficiency *in terms of human satisfaction*.

If society can produce a superabundance for no current input, this is clearly a profit of "one superabundance". In order to distribute this profit to the shareholders (the citizen inheritors of this industrial know-how), a rocket scientist would no doubt calculate the number of tickets required to distribute it, create them, and distribute them equally to all (if he were a democrat). The owners of the plant, now able to sell their products, would no doubt receive an additional dividend and liquidate some of the debt raised to build the plant. Ensuing cycles of production would be treated likewise.

The Third Age of Man will begin modestly (most probably) when some country issues a small national dividend aimed at funding some small part of a deficiency of purchasing power. That such deficiencies are continually generated is now universally accepted in all nations, as none fail to increase their money existent every year. In normal years they do this by above 10%.

Thus far, the policy towards meeting a situation in which we cannot buy society's product with the money available to us, is in large measure, to finance the building of an even greater productive capacity. This distributes wages with which to buy today's product. It also transfers the cost of today's wages onto tomorrow's greater capacity. The alternatives here are either to consume like hoggish lunatics to keep it all going, or to starve in recession because consumption, while adequate for human needs, is inadequate for financial needs (when orthodox).

The opponents of economic democracy see it in dramatic terms, where at some point, with a tumultuous shout the workers down tools, descend upon the closest warm beaches, and live out their lives in dissipation, indulgence, sloth and gluttonous irresponsibility.

On the contrary, the workers believe that dividends are only for rich people, and that such as they could never aspire to live in a society in which all progressively, and increasingly, participated in a National Dividend. Labour Leaders tug the forelock at their Bankers for maintaining work (which they represent) as the lot of man. Conservative Leaders tug the forelock before their Bankers, for maintaining the worker state of submission to the Bosses.

Since you have come this far, I will presume that you are either impervious to shock, or an academic psychiatrist studying madness. In either case, you, and probably only you, will be able to cope with the coming profanity. The chilling cry of the Age of Service in birth pangs is:

Workers of the world unite! You have nothing to lose but your jobs!

The extent to which a worker is in receipt of some National Dividend payments, is the exact extent to which he can desist from prostituting his working life to external impositions, and offer his services to others in love, because he is in this measure beyond the dictation of needs.

Marx always believed that the bosses were, and should be, paramount. His bosses were to be appointed by government, instead of privately, with increased powers because there could only be one employer in the Government.

The loss of jobs will not happen with cataclysmic suddenness. It is a remorseless, irresistible glacial process which will free men from work, despite the "everybody must work all the time" brigade forever eulogising full employment. Mondayitis may be a forgotten affliction in coming generations.

The Swiss are now (2013) in the throes of holding a referendum which if passed, will guarantee every citizen a reasonably comfortable minimum income, irrespective of all other considerations.[3] Whether passed or not, and whether financed in the right way or not, this is part of the aforesaid glacial shift which is carrying us all towards less employment. Indeed, many may kick and scream, tearing their hair as they lament the demise of the despot demanding that we serve for lucre, but still, the caravan will ever move on.

Whoever said: "Blessed are the meek: for they shall inherit the earth"?

---

3. Author's update: this referendum was not passed on this occasion.

DEFINING OBSCURITIES

I was once a member of a debating team which had considerable success by turning every contest into a "definition debate". By this we meant extending the opposition's stated case to the utmost degree, exaggerating and enlarging what we alleged they needed to prove until, hopefully, it was both ridiculous and incontestable, and thus indefensible. On the other hand, we so defined what we said we had to prove, limiting and reducing it, and confining it tightly until it amounted to a contention so very limited that our case was unassailable; a lay-down misère.

In our first major contest we were given the affirmative of the topic "That the emancipation of women has been wasted". We took control of the definition of what the topic meant immediately.

Our first affirmative speaker opened with an incontestable statement: "Milk is milk!" Then "A tanker of milk is milk, a gallon of milk is milk, and a drop of milk is milk.

"If we say that milk has been wasted, what we are saying is that milk has been wasted.

"An ocean of milk may not have been wasted, nor a ship load, but if just a drop has been incontestably wasted, and of course it has, then our case is proven."

This was the type of approach we invariably took. The rebuttal of this is to contend in-the-main, on balance, reasonably considered etc. that women's emancipation has not been wasted. To this argument from the negative side, we would respond: "So you admit it has been wasted, yes you admit it, but you wish now to quibble that it wasn't much, not too much, or not all of it. If we accused you of being a thief, do you think you could defend yourself effectively by saying 'Not much'?"

The moral of the story is that if you are to enter into public debate, take care in defining the contested issue. Its correct definition will decide more than half of the outcome. Debating undefined obscurities is a zero-sum game.

Perhaps even the majority of political disputation revolves around the "left/right" dichotomy. This debate centres upon a spectrum of political colours, and a false one. A spectrum is supposed to graduate from one thing to another, and often to its opposite: from small to large, from light to dark, from acid to alkaline for example. The political "spectrum" in most common use is not a spectrum at all.

It graduates on the extreme left from totalitarianism (communism) to the extreme right, which is also totalitarianism, in the form of Nazism. If both ends of this graduated political spectrum are the same, what is in the middle? Indeed, nothing but totalitarianism is possible anywhere on this spectrum. You can place yourself anywhere you like on this one, and you cannot but arrive at the same place. Those who see total government as the great hope obviously devised this. Only a radical redefinition of the political spectrum can save us from our favourite form of tyranny.

If the political spectrum is to depict the alternate roles for government, and we are to put Communism with its total government at the far-left end, then the far right should be its opposite, that is, no government at all, or anarchism. Few would be found at the extremities, and most would inhabit the wide-ranging centre. Certainly, this option only presents choice as to the size of government in our lives, and irrespective of size there are other considerations.

When we try to resist the temptation of using the political spectrum as a means of abuse of one's designated opponents, another construction may present itself. Politics is largely done, at least at the street level, in a manner somewhat resembling the tribalism of football supporters, so conceding honesty and fairness to the "others", even where it exists, is tantamount to betrayal. Still, pitching against the odds, I will try it.

The thing that brings people to the left is, again and again, compassion. Yes, the leadership may be charlatans and con-artists and worse, or perhaps not, but the fact is that the left sees themselves as being for and seeking a more compassionate society. In the midst of a rising crescendo of dispute and conjecture, let us suppose that at the extreme left there is the greatest density and intensity of compassion for the "under-dog".

If that can be done, then what of the right? They see themselves as champions of personal sovereignty. Freedom of speech, the rights of enterprise, personal protection through law and order, and freedom from undue regulation are among their hot points. Against charges of self-serving self-interest, exploitative practices, taking advantage of the less fortunate, all of which are true to some degree, the objective of enshrining personal sovereignty gathers its followers to the banner.

At this point, about all that will save me is a miracle. Let us suppose that one has happened. The right has conceded that the left is ahead on the issue of compassion, and the left has admitted that the right is stronger in defending personal sovereignty.

Again, we have not arrived at a true spectrum in this new one. The thing is what it is. It doesn't go as it should from one thing to its opposite, but metamorphosises in between somewhere, with compassion becoming personal sovereignty at its opposite end, and vice versa. I am not holding that this is how it should be, but simply that this is the way it actually is. So how are the morally responsible supposed to place themselves into this? Are we to compromise on compassion or on personal sovereignty?

Since it is not a true spectrum with a straight adjoining line, I am going to take some liberties with it. I am damned if I'm going to abandon either compassion or personal sovereignty. I intend to have both or nothing. Mine is a violent solution, though only affected against, and at the expense of, abstract conceptions.

I intend taking the left and arcing it 180 degrees to the north and doing the same with the right. This done I shall be standing in a perfect circle with the two ends of complete compassion and perfect personal sovereignty adjacent to each other and touching at the north. If these are opposites, and they are supposed to attract, I will try to broker a marriage. From the perspective of those within the circle the left will still be on the left, and the right on the right so there is no loss of identity, though we have bumped their heads together.

It seems to me the next most important thing to do, and this out of compassion, is to find some personal sovereignty for the left. With many not owning their own homes, dependent upon public transport, and having low incomes, a review of their neglected assets is surely in order. Brushing aside the veils, what is the greatest asset that any of us have? It is our membership in our human communities and cultures. Without this there can be absolutely nothing. So, to what does this entitle us? The answer is pretty much nothing, but this can be changed.

Every year in advanced nations, the consumer products produced and sold are more than the payments of income to people to induce them to do this production. This is always solved by increasing our debt to the banking system which creates and initially owns all of our money.

When an election is needed, we create ballot papers, and since our right to use them is based on our common membership in our countries, we all are given one each to cast our choice.

If we can marry the concepts of the two paragraphs above, we may have the seeds of a reconciliation between left and right. If needed money supply increases were distributed as are ballots, with all receiving an equal amount and no need to repay them, the meek would largely reign over consumption, and not in simply enjoying it, but in dictating their preferences which industry would be bound to obey or go bankrupt, and in this they would now largely be the proprietors of the economy. Justice for the proletariat (those without property) is in their emergence as proprietors with directive power over what production is required, and its delivery to them as their inheritance from the industrial capital of knowhow.

The abiding objection to compassion from the right, has always been in its cost. They have mistakenly thought that money, in the most part, must come from them; a natural enough assumption coming from pride. The truth is that no money whatever comes from the community; it all comes from its original manufacturers; the Banking System. They own it all, insist upon its return, and demand an increase by way of interest be returned in addition thereto. The right is totally subject to this, as is the left.

Can the compassion of the right be extended to giving them (the less fortunate, that is) access to any new and needed money creations? Since it will not be coming from their own pockets, are there prospects here of agreement?

We are not proposing any additional money creations, but simply that those money creations which now regularly and constantly take place, be distributed differently. Instead of financing increases in consumption with debt, it can be done with a national dividend if we wish it.

There are technicalities here. Money for production will still be done as debt to ensure that it can earn more than it consumes in its production; the insurance against inefficient enterprises enduring. Measuring the insufficiency of consumer funding has been many times addressed in my other essays, so it will not be pursued here. If we dare to grasp the policy of distributing the right of economic choice (money) on the same basis as political choice (ballot papers) the details can follow later. They are not "rocket science".

It is true that in defining obscurities we predetermine conclusions. It is not so much a case of cheating, but rather that all is fair in love and war. If we wish to reinvent the answer, we first have to reinvent and redefine the question. If we content ourselves with running back and forth upon the spectrum of "total government" in both directions, no other arrival is possible as a destination.

If we will compromise neither with increasing compassion, nor with defending personal sovereignty for all, we have to disarm the questions which compel it, reformulate the arena in which the contest will be decided, and take in charge the definition of the topic in debate. So then, where are we now?

Some at least will insist upon being in the middle, fairly in the radical centre of our full cycle spectrum, insisting that the "left" and the "right" hold hands and fruitfully propagate both compassion and sovereignty for persons. And there is a little bonus which comes with this.

All those of this position are the most radical, the strongest in extremism, and the only ones uncompromised in advancing the aspirations of every faction. In the end, what can you do with this, except nail it to a tree?

EGO; ERGO ERROR

One of the most comical practices of man is in his proclamations of feel-good ideas as truths. The self is thus self-destructive, the ego therefore erroneous.

One much favoured by the prideful and held to be axiomatic is *"there is no such thing as a free feed."* So let us take our average urban male and make him pay as he is pleased to tell us that he does. He has disallowed himself from receiving sunshine or air and is disqualified from even standing space as he has created none of these, and thus in a proper sense, has not paid for them.

OK, but he has paid, at least, for last night's dinner of apple pie. So, he conceived of and invented the apple tree did he, domesticated wheat, and discovered fire?

"Oh, but he has paid others for his feed", simply will not work. If there is no such thing as something for nothing, it cannot be allowed to anybody else either. So, unless we can find someone who has created sunshine, air and the three dimensions, discovered fire, and invented language and wheat and apple trees, there is no one with whom we may trade to pay for them.

Ultimately there may in fact be one feed which is unavoidably allowed as being free to man. If we strip from him all that is a consequence of his inheritance, our urban male will not have benefit of his city, nor his tools or even his weapons. He may discover a cave but will have no means of capturing a duck or a rabbit for dinner. The one free feed he may chance upon in these circumstances, is carrion. This is a free feed which, once he is hungry enough, he will be pleased to acknowledge as it might be a very long time until the next one.

Please understand that I am fully in favour of something for nothing. Is there another way, when nothing at all can be paid for in any absolute sense? If there is anything for which we must inevitably pay, it is most likely to be prideful statements.

I can beat my chest and proclaim that I have never had anything for nothing, and the price I will pay for this is in the demonstration of my profound and abiding ignorance, and the exultation of my status as an ignoramus.

Some men earn money by serving others who already have some of it, and some acquire it by inheritance or at the roulette wheel in a casino, but apparently our ego is best served by stating that "*we made money*". This is not just boastful; it is downright criminal. Counterfeiting carries long prison sentences, though fortunately, telling lies when not under oath does not, so together with the fact that nobody believes what we are saying in this instance, the falsehood can continue quite unabated and uncorrected.

The concept of *the self-made man* is another egotism without foundation. His parents would have had something to do with his being, one would think, but that he "made himself" in other respects is equally farcical. No matter how little help he may have had from others, did he live in a community without language, the division of labour, tools, or productive knowhow and technologically advantageous processes?

Man is a social being and he lives in a cooperative community. We are all interdependent; important though our independence is and should be to us, it is always a relative thing. Has ever a man lived who did not contribute to the making of our culture? He may have but coined a phrase, invented a recipe, offered a useful suggestion, created a garden, said a kind word, given "a hand", or done a good turn. Culture is an organic construct built of our innumerable forebears' contributions. In summation, no man is an island.

Others are present in every success. Even Robinson Crusoe took with him to his island a knowledge of how to do things which was not of his own invention.

Without this he could never have survived, remarkable and praiseworthy though his achievement was.

So, while we should honour those who have succeeded against the odds and in the face of great difficulties, the context of every man's triumph is in community. We concede this in some areas of life, and in others we do not.

In the 21st century we allow that every person is a rightful stakeholder in his community politically. All get the political vote. We each get an equal share of them. In corporate elections, each gets votes representative of his or her stake holding in the company.

In the economy however, the communal stake holding is not acknowledged. When additional money is needed to facilitate additional exchange require-ments, it is simply created. There is no other way of doing it. With these dollars, now costlessly created in cyberspace, with each representing a right to elect a measure of consumption, there is no communal distribution. All go only to those who will accept it as debt. A type of ballot paper which confers the right to consume, although this right is conditional upon not consuming a like amount at some point in the future.

In funding production this is just. If one borrows for production, it is reasonable to insist that he obtain at least a like amount from sales and repay his loan, or inefficient production will burgeon in the economy.

There are circumstances however, now more or less permanent, in which an increase in the purchasing power of consumers is the objective of increasing the money supply. Allowing this on the sole basis that future consumption will be curtailed by a like amount, is a form of madness. It disenfranchises the community, the very owner of the productive ability of said community, and enslaves it in ever-increasing debt.

When a community has produced more consumer goods than it has been paid incomes, it is in profit, and distributing this profit as repayable debt is like charging shareholders for the dividend they are due.

Thus, we are back to the original vanity, *there is no such thing as a free dividend.* The corporate world would simply not put up with it, and nor should they. The community needs to play catchup.

IT MAY ONLY TAKE ONE

One, on its own, has often proved to be a sufficiency. The revolutionary Lenin once said that "The fewer the better, provided that the fewer are better." On this at least I agree with him. As the fewest of persons or anything else is obviously "one", it might be interesting to look at what one has done.

James Watt gave us the first working engine. This engine gave rise to all of its descendants; from hydrocarbon powered internal combustion ones, to nuclear powered steam driven turbines.

Nikola Tesla gave us alternating current (AC) electricity. Even now we are still filling in the spaces as to where and how this may be applied.

There are very few heroes in my consternation of planetary importances, but I am pleased to report that at least one of them was both ridiculously wrong, and the instigator of intellectually world changing developments. How and why?

He was an ancient Greek and he hypothesised that all matter was composed of water. His name was Thales, and he argued his case well enough to set this quandary loose amongst the intellectuals of his day. The key to his brilliance was that he asked a hitherto unasked question; of what is matter composed? Those who wished to show that he was wrong soon hypothesised that rather, everything came from earth, air, fire and water; and this was the majority consensus for some centuries.

It also, quite amazingly, inspired the hypothesis that all was composed of atoms. We are still dissecting this into quirks and a plethora of subatomic particles. It was Thales who kicked this into the cosmos of our awareness.

So what might happen if one, in this case one nation, decided to change everything? The suggestion involves neither violence, confrontation, nor any antagonism towards others.

What would happen if Russia chose to do a comprehensive set of national accounts?

I have nominated Russia because its President, Vladimir Putin, made a speech in Munich on the 10th of February 2007, making it plain that neither he nor Russia would countenance a "unipolar world". At that time he had not "blotted his copybook" as happened later, and his options in resisting the "one-worlders" were completely open.

The impetus towards a unipolar world is wholly driven by a private monopoly towards globalism, and this through their sanction over money creations. No private persons create money and the laws against counterfeiting enforce this, nor does any Government create it as their budgets evidence none of this. Money is the preserve of the "Golden Internationale" which creates, distributes, and owns it, and the future of the human organism is as they would nominate it to be. Those who would repudiate this will need to nominate an alternate source of this thing which is "money".

If any nation decides that this is not OK, and that the best construction of sanctions is multipolar and dispersed, and that subsidiarity (the notion that governance functions are best employed closest to the people affected) because this is most conducive to delivering human satisfaction, this will change everything.

So back to poor besmirched Russia. What would happen if it really did decide to reconstruct the world on the basis that all nations were free and endowed with self-determination? You're suggesting that the sinner become a saint? Of course, that is where all saints have come from – there is no other source of them to be had.

The answer to what would happen at some levels, is... not much. Legislation, regulations, and most of our modus operandi would barely notice.

All that we would have initially changed is that one nation would have chosen to do a set of books. Thales may have approved.

If Russia had done a comprehensive set of national accounts this would probably have raised eyebrows nowhere. But what if, through their influence, others were caused to follow? If Brazil, Nicaragua, Zambia, Turkey, Bolivia, Syria, Iran, and India did it, what would we learn?

We may discover as per the prototype accounts done at the following link, that they have some utility: http://www.socialcredit.com.au/uploads/NationalAccountsPrototype.pdf

The optimum increase or issue of money might just be relative to economic reality.

If it ever came to pass that money issued might be equated to a measured insufficiency of purchasing power in the hands of consumers, and only to this, and that this were directly addressed, the sanction empowering the unipolar impetus towards a centrally directed world would atrophy.

If these National Accounts were done in several countries, eventually someone may suggest - since we are profitable and a deficiency of purchasing power has to be made good - that the money created to do this might be thought of as a dividend payable to citizens rather than as a debt owing to bankers.

The push for a unipolar world will atrophy once it doesn't have the support of everything that costlessly created money can buy.

The above requires Putin, or in the Constantine model, at least some Christian prince somewhere, getting his bloody head into gear.

REALTY AND FINANCIAL REALITY

U ntil Robert Ardrey published his work *The Territorial Imperative*, the obsessive urge to acquire real estate was generally regarded as a trait of humanity. It is; but one we share with all creatures. As Ardrey showed, mammals, birds, insects and even worms compete to acquire the advantage of space.

For decades this has been the foundational urge upon which our "capitalist system," has been built and maintained. How?

Since at least the 1920's it has been realised by those who administer capitalism (the bankers) and the rare few who intelligently observe them doing it, that industrial accounting has a recurring problem. *Costs and prices are generated at a rate faster than are the personal incomes needed to meet them.* No, I am not here going to attempt a proof. Later perhaps, but you will probably need to accept this as a working hypothesis if the rest of this essay is to make sense.

My Australian National Profit and Loss Account of March 2022 (see chapter entitled *A National Supply and Demand Account*, page 189) shows that the production of consumer products amounted to over $11,000 more per person than the personal incomes distributed to buy them. The problem then became how to find and inject into the economy an additional amount approximating $11,000 per person each year to allow sufficient product to be sold to keep the economy out of recession. For decades there has been a ready answer practiced.

Lending was increased to prospective home buyers until the deficiency of purchasing power was approximated by increased debt money. In countries such as the UK, the US, and Australia, up to two-thirds of all the money which now exists began its life as a loan for residential housing.[1] This practice of continually inflating residential real estate continues today. Total indebtedness to the credit issuing banking system is the main means of funding the annual increase in the money supply needed to keep our form of capitalist economy liquid and endowed with a sufficiency of purchasing power to continue and minimise recession.

The realisation that this is the situation began with the writings of C H Douglas and his associates, beginning from about 1919. Douglas's suggestion was that when the community's purchasing power was measured, and if found to be inadequate, that a National Dividend be declared and paid to citizens as their proprietary right. Banks would continue to finance production to the extent that they wished and were prepared to take responsibility for it, but they would not be permitted to finance consumption increases by increasing the money supply.

In today's figures as per the National Profit and Loss Account of 2022 quoted above, annual national dividends paid would approximate $44,000 for each family of four persons.

This of course, opens the question of what policy should be adopted to finance residential dwellings henceforth?

The first principle here is that banks would not be permitted to finance housing consumption through money supply increases. They would not be inhibited from financing residential constructions, but financing their use (consumption as it were) would be done otherwise.

Here a number of policy changes are needful.

---

1. The Bank of England's website gives the money supply (M4) as of October 2016 and "lending secured on dwellings" as 2,250,436 and 1,318,911 million pounds respectively, the latter being by that time 58.6% of all UK money in existence.

The traditional "Building Societies" once more prolific than now, did not create additional money in financing housing. Depositors surrendered funds to these societies which became the building society's deposits in the banks. These funds were used to finance the public to purchase homes quite independently from the banks themselves. They used existing money, not newly created additional money to do so.

Some persons limited their consumption by saving with Building Societies, and others increased their consumption by taking these funds as loans.

By this means the banks can be prohibited from appropriating the national dividend due to citizens by financing housing consumption with money creations. Making interest received by depositors in building societies tax free may be a useful policy option.

Other initiatives may be added.

I make no apology for taking a distributist approach here. A healthy society requires the widest possible distribution of property throughout society. The greater the ownership of homes by the families occupying them the greater the general level of responsibility in that society. This is not a policy of taking from Peter to assist Paul, but rather, of instituting policy towards greater and more widespread participation and ownership as a practical policy.

The not so small matter of the $44,000 which would go to each average family each year debt free, and as a dividend payable upon their proprietary interest in their country would answer many a difficulty in encouraging home ownership. Saving would be assisted as would paying the rent while they do so.

Diverting the banks efforts from deliberately inflating house prices to funding their production would of course, greatly aid the supply of housing.

Adding $44,000 per annum to consumer incomes as an alternative to adding it to consumer debt, would, at least in my opinion, completely reorientate society. The possibility of paying off $44,000 of debt each year would markedly reduce family financial stress, and leave us more time for helping each other.

Of course, paying a national dividend of $44,000 and also allowing the banks to continue inflating house prices by a like amount would be highly inflationary.

We would be sending $2 to purchase $1 of product. We have to choose between funding consumption in either the one way or the other.

Other initiatives need not be neglected.

Currently, allowing families in rural and semi-rural locations to donate an acre or two to other family members for separate dwellings is inhibited by many regulations. Why? They usually provide their own water and septic systems at no community cost and build their own access roads. Infrastructure such as is essential in urban areas is not required. Practical measures to assist residential home building make sense. As technology allows working from home easier, why are we limiting escaping to the country?

Of course, all this could go much further. The cost of providing infrastructure to congested urban areas is known. As a community economy, could we not pay those who choose to live beyond the sprawling cities an amount equal to half the savings we enjoy because they do it?

Thinking about society and its conditions, needs to go beyond that favoured by current banking policy. If we cannot confront the current policy of allowing the banking system to steal the need for increased consumer purchasing power by their imposition of ever-increasing debt, we will have to postpone the future.

What DMC will Mean for Banking

With the coming of DMC, banks will not be permitted to make loans for consumption. This will be funded through a National Dividend, issued in equal parts to all people. The amount of the National Dividend which is necessary will be carefully calculated in a National Profit and Loss Account.

Banks will, however, continue to freely finance production. Funds for this will be provided from the National Credit Authority, the NCA, and will be repayable to the NCA upon the maturity of the loans. No interest will be charged to the banks for these funds for production. The one and only condition upon which these funds are provided to the banks, will be that the banks take responsibility for them. If loans for production default, then the losses will be made up from shareholders' funds. If they are profitably managed, the profits will accrue to the shareholders.

The banks' Balance Sheets after DMC will be simpler. Money owed to the NCA to make productive loans will be their liabilities, and outstanding loans for production which are in good standing (not in default) will be their assets. Banks' balance sheets in this respect should actually balance.

However, in the interim, once DMC is instituted the banks' Balance Sheets will have deposits arising from three different sources. Some of their deposits will have resulted from their own lending prior to DMC being instituted. Some will have arisen from the NCA paying national dividends. Some will have occurred because the NCA has funded the banks to make productive loans. This will mean that changes are necessary in how banks do their balance sheets during this interim period.

Prior to DMC their loans will have been accounted as their assets, and all their deposits as liabilities. Since every loan created a deposit when spent, and every loan when repaid cancelled out a deposit of that amount, loans and deposits balanced. When the NCA pays out National Dividends and finances banks' productive loans, and they are paid into bank accounts, banks' liabilities (their deposits) will increase by this amount.

For example, if on day one of DMC banks assets (their loans) total $100 million, and their liabilities (their deposits) total $100 million they are in balance. However, once the NCA pays a National Dividend and issues credit to fund banks' productive loans, of say $7 million and $3 million respectively, when these are deposited into the banks their liabilities (their deposits) are then $10 million ($3 million plus $7 million) greater than their assets and total $110 million.

To meet this situation the $10 million which arose from the NCA's payments will also be accounted as assets held in trust for the NCA. Assets are thus now $110 million, and they equal the banks' liabilities of $110 million.

Incorporating this into each banks' balance sheet is easy enough. In this case 10% of deposits have arisen from the action of the NCA in creating money. If one bank has deposits of $37 million, $3.7 million will be added to their assets, as being held in trust for the NCA. If the other banks' assets were $63 million, then $6.3 million will be added to their assets in the same way. In this way if the banks' deposits and liabilities were each in total $100 million on day one, on day two they will each be $110 million.

Apart from the right to finance consumption, the banks have suffered no disadvantage.

DMC does however offer some major advantages to the banks. The banks liabilities to each other in the clearing houses will end. To explain; currently, if a bank deposit is withdrawn from Bank A and deposited in Bank B, then Bank A owes that amount to Bank B. This can only be met either by Bank A attracting a like amount of deposits from Bank B, or by parting with shareholders' funds.

At present this is a considerable constraint upon bank lending. Banks can and do now create money by making loans, but this can only be done in unison with other banks and in proportion to their market presence.

Suppose there are two banks in a country. Bank X has two thirds of the business, and Bank Y but one third. Bank X has two thirds of the customers, deposits, and loans outstanding and Bank Y but half this.

Suppose that a single large loan is made. If Bank X makes a loan of $3 million, on average only $2 million of the deposits this causes will be made back into Bank X. One third, or $1 million of this loan will go into Bank Y. Then Bank X owes Bank Y $1 million which drains shareholders' funds.

If Bank Y makes the $3 million loan, then two thirds, or $2 million goes into Bank X, and Bank Y owes this amount to the other Bank. This is solved by lending in unison.

If Bank X loans out $6 million and Bank Y only half this much, or $3 million, each will get the same amount back on deposit as they have loaned, and neither will owe the other. Bank X will get deposits of $4 from its own loan, and $2 million from Bank Y's loan, or $6 million in all. Bank Y will get $2 million from Bank X's loan, and $1 million from its own, or $3 million in all. Each bank's deposits and loans are equal.

This is the real constraint upon bank lending in the system prior to DMC, numerous contrary assertions notwithstanding. The $100 million in deposits which were present on day one of the DMC system will be of two kinds. One kind will have been loaned by the banks for consumption prior to DMC. These will never be increased or renewed once paid. They will therefore atrophy with repayments until they are nil. They will be repaid from deposits either arising from an NCA origin or from the lending actions of the banks prior to DMC.

That part of the $100 million in deposits on day one of DMC which were loaned for productive purposes will be accounted as assets held in trust for the NCA. In this way they will not be net liabilities to the banks.

After DMC is instituted, banks' loans, which will all be for production, will be financed by the NCA. Where the deposits go and to which banks will be irrelevant. They will have an obligation to repay the NCA when the loans for production fall due, but none to each other.

After all loans originally loaned out for consumption are repaid and thus cancelled out of existence, the interim period of accounting will be ended.

Deposits held on behalf of others will not be permitted to be accounted as either bank assets or liabilities. Deposits have value to their owners as a record of their right to make claims against others, though they have no intrinsic value. They will henceforth be records kept in cyberspace and administered by banks as a service to others. Their shareholders' funds held in their accounts will obviously be their assets.

This renders bank deposits as obsolete to the banks' purposes. They will have no interest at all in attracting them except for charging service charges upon them. They will certainly not pay any interest on deposit balances.

So will receiving interest upon your money be abolished? Not at all. This too will operate in a different way.

Non-bank financial institutions, such as building societies or credit unions, will offer interest for your deposits. You may transfer your funds to these, and your deposit will become part of a Building Society's bank deposit, for example. The Building Society will then administer your payments and receipts, and most account administration will fall to them if most people do this.

As banks will henceforth be forbidden to make loans for the purposes of consumption, personal loans, financing residential housing, and funding other consumption will be off limits to Banks. Banks will continue to finance housing construction and consumer production as much as they please, but not their use.

In this way, people who forego personal consumption, even temporally, by putting their money into a non-bank financial organisation will make it available to others. No new money creation will henceforth be available for the purposes of consumption, as this will be fully funded by the National Dividend going to everyone. No double funding of consumption will be available to finance inflation.

The practice of raising interest rates to limit consumption or lowering them to encourage it, will neither be practiced nor needed.

A building society may perhaps be owned by a bank but will not be permitted to make loans other than from funds in the building society's bank account. Money creation other than by the NCA will have ended.

In fact, the banks will be much more secure under DMC than they are now. Why?

Banks fail when, after a lending spree compelled upon them to compete with the other banks, a shock is administered to the economy. This shock may come in the form of a bursting housing bubble, a war, or a stock market crash. In the rush of everyone to protect themselves by transferring their funds to elsewhere, some banks are left with more obligations to other banks than they have from them. The others refuse to "play with them" anymore, and they can no longer operate; a Lehman Brothers event, as it were, then occurs.

A bankers' instincts are traditionally cautious and conservative. If he is insulated from the panic attacks of other banks, has all his loans financed by the NCA to any extent he will take responsibility for them, and this at no interest, receives service fees on all accounts, pays no interest on deposits, and has no responsibility or risks from consumer lending, he is much more secure than he was prior to DMC.

All the bankers need to do here is to get a sober understanding of DMC and then cooperate in achieving it in their own self-interest.

THE BEAN BREEDERS

I nto the 20th Century, whole legions of bean counters marched through industry and commerce, disciplining the indolent and indulging the diligent. It was not the legions, but rather the ledgers, which imposed the pax universal across human endeavour.

Their rule was peculiar to its own medium. Whether it was better to produce six items of popular utility which lasted for only five years each, or one which endured for 30 years, was determined wholly by the counting of beans. The impact of building in obsolescence upon the environment, for instance, by consuming multiple resources instead of fewer, did not compute. How many beans went in, how many came out, and over what time, was thought the sole determinant of well-being of the human organism and economy. Why?

This question was met with incredulity, for its answer was self-evident and indeed, axiomatic. The limiting factor governing human endeavour was everywhere undoubtedly, and unarguably, beans. If you had them people would respond to your expressed will, if you did not, they would not. Beans were to all things, obviously, as is the universe to oblivion.

Of course, I will concede that measuring costs and received values is a functional necessity in any economy. We need to know whether, in consuming two units of value in a productive endeavour, the product attained has a value of four units, or only one. In the first instance we can do it again and often, and in the last it is destructive of value, and if sufficiently repeated, of the whole economy.

The bean counters, while everywhere credited with near absolute powers of determination in things economic, were, from another perspective, merely the musterers and minders of the cattle of another. Beans were neither born, nor did they expire, as a result of being counted. They all came from somewhere beyond the horizons and farthest perspectives of the incumbent counters. The beans in question here were units of credit, and credit is, in turn, the substance of things hoped for, the evidence of things unseen.

In more primitive societies grain, salt or metals substituted for beans, but with greater sophistication any widely recognised claim upon others - such as bank deposits which existed wholly in cyberspace - were accounted beans. These beans were formless, enumerated abstractions; wraiths acknowledged as powerful and omnipotent in the minds of men, though undiscoverable in any fixed physical form.

Money or mammon was now a child of the imagination; a thing of the spirit, a product of faith, an ethereal being (or bean). The really wonderful thing for bankers was that now money could be brought into being by a process which can only be described as one of miraculous concept.

The process of creating artificial claims and loaning them out on the one simple basis that people would accept them, is ancient in origin. The cuneiforms of the Sumerians were invented and used primarily, it is believed, to record debts and receipts. Once the clay tablets were accepted as valid and worthy of faith, their credit (from the Latin *credo:* I believe) was the basis of issuing more credit or breeding this particular form of "beans". This practice descended in various forms and through multiple countries, and found pretty much universal application.

For our purposes we shall take it up in England in the 17th Century. The founder of modern bean breeding was one William Paterson. Born in Scotland in 1655, he fled under a cloud to England in 1672, and thence to the Bahamas becoming a wealthy merchant, where the New World Encyclopaedia reports the rumour of his "keeping close connections with pirates".

He returned to Europe and attempted to find support for his "Darien" scheme. This involved the trade of the Pacific and Atlantic oceans going to Panama, where the goods would somehow be transhipped across the isthmus. He eventually tried to achieve this with Scottish support in 1698 but it failed miserably. Malaria was part of his problems.

Meanwhile he had conceived the idea and successfully promoted his proposal for a "Bank of England". During the time of the Stuart Kings, Parliament was weary of banking suggestions. The fear was that the Kings may be provided with a means of evading Parliament's control of supply, that is, the supply of funds to the King's purposes.

Paterson promoted the bank with such advocacy as "The Bank shall hath benefit of interest upon all moneys which it createth out of nothing." By 1694, with the Stuarts deposed and the proposed Bank ostensibly to be established under Parliamentary control, the Bank was founded. Paterson was a director for a time before being removed by his fellow directors for what has been variously reported as either a disagreement or a scandal.

Looking back 400 plus years, the idea that a parliament could control a bank is rather fanciful. Parliaments are, after all, simply large committees of persons intent upon self-promotion, and with no interest in understanding the vagaries of money creation, outside of a resolve to get some of it. Because politicians will not apply themselves to understanding banking and its awesome prerogatives, they end in submission. In all the areas that bankers choose to think sufficiently important, they have ever controlled the politicians.

Their chief means of control is through their overwhelming ownership or financial entrapment and direction of the media. The media does not need to tell us what to think, of course; it just tells us what to think about. By controlling the agenda, and with the propensity of every public to conform because believing what most others believe is acclaimed as virtue, the controller of the media and its banking suzerainty, not parliament, sets the agenda.

For the next 300 years the culture of the bean breeders determined a policy of industrial might (the object of the industrial revolution) and political hegemony (the object of the British Empire).

The next prominent bean breeder to be examined is one Montagu Norman. He became a Director of the Bank of England in 1907 and served as its Governor from 1925 to 1944. He was somewhat eccentric and obsessed with the restoration of the gold standard, and furtively travelled incognito back and forth across the Atlantic under the alias of Mr Skinner to influence its re-establishment and maintenance with such as Benjamin Strong of the Federal Reserve Bank of New York.

The British reintroduced the gold standard early in his governorship in 1925. Relating the world's credit to all the gold in existence, which constituted a cube of the metal 20x20x20 meters, was an absurdity, and this being proven, the gold standard was abandoned in the UK forever in 1931. Meanwhile the disruption to Europe's prosperity caused credit restrictions and brought extreme hardship; a major factor in Germany turning to a strongman for relief, and subsequently leading to World War II.

With the imminent collapse of the gold standard, Norman urged the founding of Central Banks in the Empire and Europe. His influence saw the establishment of the Bank of International Settlements in 1930 and the appointment of Sir Otto Niemeyer as a Director.

In this way was the control of credit moved another step further away from Parliaments and Governments. The bean breeders were in ascendance as never before.

Norman appointed an advisor, one Harry Siepmann from Treasury, and sent him to Versailles as an aid to John Maynard Keynes, and Siepmann came to largely accept Keynes's economics and subsequently influenced Norman in their acceptance too.

The salvation of economies was thus to be had in the continual provision of beans as debt from their banking breeders. Interest rates have been reduced, sometimes to negative ones, and debt ramped up via quantitative easing and other like expediencies beyond any possible bounds of repayment. Any concept that the people who created the increased wealth should participate in the ownership of consequent increased credit, and share it equitably, is a distant planet indeed.

We are now in the Fifth Century of governance through bean breeding. It is now the 427th year of enthrallment to Paterson's curse. Nery a word is breathed in the media of considering a National Dividend to distribute our artificially (and costlessly) created and communally agreed claims upon wealth, which of course, is money.

As a person far from the councils of this suzerainty, the empire seems in these late days to have contracted a degeneracy the likes of ancient Rome in its later years. It would now seem to be policy to install "woke folk" in the agencies of the bean breeder's influence, the media. They obsess about transgenderism, impossible rights instead of useful ones, climate change while ignoring the real limitations of carbon dioxide as a greenhouse gas, homosexuality, and a pandemic for which an effective cure in the form of ivermectin is available, though ignored. It seems that more of the like may be anticipated.

It is as though old-fashioned degeneracy and fear is the current policy of a governance, itself degenerate and fearful, to disorientate and confuse a populace chronically in need of meeting the impositions confronting it, in its necessity of finding a saner world.

Those whom the gods wish to destroy, they first send mad. It's time, and it's happening.

Since prophecy is the true test of science, can the world's hegemony of ascendant bean counters reach its 500th anniversary?

THE LAST FRONTIER

N apoleon only had half the story. Yes, they march on their stomachs, but they do battle with their brains. Unless you know what the key sanction in the world is, and something of the agenda of those who control it, don't even attempt to be a soldier. Stay at home, stay out of the road, and please don't attempt to help. You can't. You don't have a weapon, and only by reading the above have you started to know where all effective weapons are to be found.

If you want to make your enemy look irresistible and inevitably victorious, embark on the most popular policy amongst well-meaning souls. Determine to catch as many of the enemy's incoming missiles as you can. You will evidence your patriotism, show your determination and energy, and in case you are tempted to slacken, you will catch a few too.

Well never mind. Nobody loses them all. Catching incoming missiles (adoration and accolades notwithstanding), is the ultimate refuge of losers. Refining the range, effectiveness and frequency of the missiles is the object of the personnel at the missile launchers, who, basking in the absence of initiatives to interrupt, lessen or inhibit launching, clearly see themselves as being on the side of history.

Before the newly directed patriots turn to assail the launching pads, the armoury of the brain will need even more to be considered. Most of the launching pads are ensconced in the media. Behind these media initiatives are enclaves of "woke folk" who, mostly for the enjoyment of provocation, offer themselves in servitude.

Judging the progress of a war by counting the percentage of missiles intercepted is meaningless, when unrelated to how many continue to be launched at you. Likewise, accounting progress in terms of launching pads destroyed is irrelevant if more again are built. The scattering of enclaves of weird personnel is also only to be considered in terms of their coalescence elsewhere.

Severing heads may not only lack utility, but it may even inform the enemy of effectiveness for later initiatives. Whether there is a puppet-master, where his heart is, and what may be affected with a wooden stake, are the needful questions in dealing with a Lernaean Hydra. It is the enemy's ability to resupply in the face of losses which is relevant.

In the struggle for governance of the human organism, command of the resources of war is decided primarily by numbers, not those of useful idiots, not of media agencies, nor by incendiary ideas, but by the 'one ring' to find them, draw them near, and in the darkness bind them. Money commands all that money can buy. Here is the heart of the matter.

Again, Napoleon was wrong. In the contest for human hegemony, it is not morale, but money which is to all else as ten is to one.

Incontestably, and without dispute, the manufacture of money is to be found in the functions of current banking systems. They monopolise its creation as fait credit, own it all, distribute it only by renting it to society, insist upon its return with increase, and hold all the sanctions in nominating its recipients.

The moral resources of ordinary folk of goodwill are certainly considerable, but whatever its resolve, energy, or heroism, expending all wholly in defence against anti-social initiatives can only delay defeat. Victory necessitates an offensive to incapacitate the adversary's means of initiative. Only an offensive success can end it. So, what is the nature of this imperative?

It is a simple and innocuous thing. All it demands is truth: a determination of the truth of the nature and facts of society's money system. But how can this be discerned? It will be found in measuring it.

Fortunately, a prototype account was done for the year 2014 in the United States which reveals the nature of our dilemma.[1]

It showed that the total aggregate incomes of all Americans were $10.1 trillion. This was the total inducement paid out to cause them to deliver a total of consumer goods both produced and paid for of $12.5 trillion. Of course, this left a balance of $2.4 trillion as a profit of their economy which their incomes were insufficient to consume. This profit of their economy could only be cleared by increasing their total indebtedness by, in this case, $2.3 trillion in that year. This was done and a recession diverted, at least for now.

This $2.3 trillion was added to the national debt, now approximating $90 trillion in all, which reflects the accumulation of past profits, the access to which was only permitted through increasing indebtedness to the manufacturer of "credit", a prerogative of the banking system.

Since all money now is fiat, or virtual money, recorded in cyberspace as an enumerated abstraction as bank deposits, we are dominated and held in thrall to a wraith-like contrivance without form, and subjected to any confusion, misinformation, or device to undo common morality and sense and keep it that way.

We need only to evidence society's profitability in proper National Accounts and claim the true increment of our economic activity as a debt-free National Dividend payable equally to all of society's stakeholders - its people.

The "woke" may indeed be readily disenfranchised. Not so, the awake.

---

1. This account, both unfortunately and necessarily technical in nature, is available to those equipped, and to those not so fortunately enabled also, at: http://www.socialcredit.com.au/uploads/NationalAccountsPrototype.pdf

"ARE WE THERE YET?"

A JOURNEY TOWARDS ECONOMIC DEMOCRACY

I s it We the People who are behind the steering wheel of modern democracy? Many of us have the feeling that we're still pretty much in the back seat asking "How long now?"

A survey of 1780 revealed that only 3% of the population in England voted, and in 1831 in Scotland only 0.17% voted (4,500 in 2.6 million). Now of course everybody votes, but who is at the steering wheel?

What explains this remarkable rise in the percentage of people with votes in the last 200 years? Care is needed here. The case for "the people demanded it" is not an open and shut one. Except in a few countries where voting is compulsory, in most countries and in most elections the majority still doesn't vote. Did a lack of enthusiasm triumph?

Previous to two centuries ago, the aristocracy allied to other propertied classes ruled. Though they thought of themselves as the defenders of all society, this was not an unqualified success, to put it mildly, and was of course always done on terms of their own advantage. Nevertheless - as the defenders of folk traditions and religion, ethical norms and customs, and sometimes of prejudice best neglected - they had measured success. And then an elephant walked into the room.

The aristocracy's power was a vestige of the feudal age. When production was not mobile on roads and waterways, the local landholder owned the decisive sanction over the livelihoods of all; the goods which sustained us. With the rise of the mercantile system and the predominance of exchange, money ascended into the Kingdom of the Castle. The time for the Aristocracy to play the role of the "dirty rascal" had arrived.

Money, the possession of credit, the right to create money, distribute it only through loans, charge interest and to compound that interest, had come into its inheritance. Through the power of the mortgage, the ownership of the media, and the patronage of academia and "science", money appointed a proxy to represent it. That proxy was the majority, with the vacancies of its head filled by endless repetition from the controlled agencies of money.

So democracy triumphed, though not of itself, but as the creature of the new and more dominant aristocracy which none could recognise or even suspect, unless the origin of credit as a private (a very private) monopoly could be discerned, and be believed to exist; which, without the captive media shouting about it, was almost never. The arrogance of the ordinary fellow that he knew how the world worked rendered him impervious to being told. The media had got to his pride first.

Though it is not over yet. The world has seen many a regime supplanted; the reptile by the dinosaur, and the dinosaur by the mammal, for example. How could ordinary fellows ever supplant the power of all that money can buy? The first necessity is that enough of us give up the prestige among our fellows of *seeming to know* how power works and is exercised, and then devoting ourselves to actually finding this out.

Telling it how it is, is normally a mistake. This would be too easy to own. I used to poison dingoes with suet laced with strychnine. In open display it was treated with suspicion. Wrap it in newspaper, put it under a rock or timber somewhat off the beaten track, and make them sniff it out and work and scratch away for it, and the newspaper would be found with teeth marks. This is why it is such heavy work to change others' minds - or to change our own.

The advantage is always with those imposing the sanctions to sing a narrative in endless repetition; always, until it induces the thought "Methinks they do repeat too much". Disappointment with politics and the efficacy of voting is now a social reality. Why? I suggest it is because the choices it offers are too few, and its means of differentiating between things is too little.

The means of improving our lives are seldom political choices, that is, ones to be had through voting; anyway they come years apart, and are usually of little effect.

With every hour we elect. We elect to do or not to do, to consider or dismiss, to say or not, to go or stay, or as Shakespeare had it, to be or not to be. Actually there are two formal voting systems which are collectively organised. In one we vote either by ballot papers or electronically via the internet to appoint politicians, company directors, club officers or sporting captains. We have learned to do this democratically, the essence of which method involves each having an equal number of the "rights to choose"; we get one such "right" each per person or per share which is represented.

It is difficult to speak of the other formal voting system without shame. Shame? How? Because in this voting system nobody is given any votes at all! And more shameful than this, almost nobody chooses to notice this parsimony. Then how do we get them? We have to get them from those who already have them.

We get them from others through serving; a wage system. We get them from others by giving of our substance; surrendering our assets, our goods or services. OK, so we get them from others who have had them from others. That will work. Of course it will work. But it only works if ultimately, in the final analysis, they are had from others who did not have them at all. Otherwise they don't and can't exist, of course.

With money, the economic vote, we elect the means of living; the means of sustenance, of entertainment, of shelter, of learning and informing the spirit. This is the great ballot, the election of life in all its aspects, but in this poll, this plebiscite, we are given no votes at all. All have to be obtained from those others who don't have them at all, but own the means of creating them out of nothing. These others, as policy, do not distribute them democratically with all sharing freely and equally.

This is not democracy. It is an overlordship of such despotism, such un-recognised power, and such all-pervasive sanctions, as to paint all previous aris-tocracies as but puny and anaemic custodians of social policy.

The measured addition to money votes in existence in the United States in 2014 was $2.3 trillion. That is, money created in addition to that which existed at the beginning of that year. While this amounted to $7,500 per person or $30,000 per family of four, none at all was given to those who own that country: its citizens.[1] Even social security was taken from others via taxation.

Though 98% of this money was not printed, but created in cyberspace and this done costlessly on a keyboard, none was distributed costlessly to its owners as are other votes and ballots.

All was created and its ownership retained in the banking houses chartered to do this. It served as their means of manning the steering wheel of the social organism, and directing it to the means and objectives, policies and values consistent, primarily, with their own self- interest.

As the back seat passengers in this vehicle of human destiny, what may we do? We can make it plain that we want a destiny of democracy. And not just the little one of political democracy (which is overawed and currently the captive of money and its suborned media) but the big one which is economic democracy too!

Firstly, we need to make it plain that we want a destination of economic democracy. "We want economic democracy! We want economic democracy!"

Secondly, "Are we there yet? Are we there yet? Are we there yet?"

Who are they, that command the world's money-creation function, that they will forever *give their son a stone?*

---

1. A detailed exposition of this may be had at http://www.socialcredit.com
   .au/uploads/NationalAccountsPrototype.pdf

PART THREE

Essays from off the wall, out of left field, and beyond the expected

AN ENIGMATIC DREAMER

J ohn Lennon sang "You may say I'm a dreamer, but I'm not the only one."

My dilemma is somewhat different. *I told myself that I was dreaming, and since then I have never been able to decide whether I was dreaming or not.*

It all resulted from a long chain of experiences and circumstances. My brother and I had bought a large tract of virgin land and were attempting to turn it into an operating cattle station. We were in debt up to our necks, and then some, and we took the drilling rig we had to provide watering points for the cattle on our property, and went contract drilling with it.

Creature comforts did not fit into our modus operandi. The truck-mounted rig was loaded almost beyond endurance with drill stems, pumps, jackhammers and other equipment. The four-wheel drive vehicle pulled the compressor trailer. The back of this "ute" contained every other conceivable necessity for drilling in totally isolated locations. Into this we somehow deposited a cardboard carton with a change of clothes each, (there were only the two of us), and another with a frying pan and sundry cans of food. These austere provisions were the only compromises we were prepared to make to our load, to provide the means of life support. We worked and lived like this for three months.

On one occasion it took us two days to drive twenty miles from one hole to the next drilling site. It was over sandy country in the dry season, and we dry-bogged every few hundred meters. We dug out the truck wheels, put saplings between the dual wheels, and then went a little further. When it got dark, we threw down the shovels, quaffed down a can of food, threw down a sheet of canvas and slept on it as the only bedding to be had. When it became light, we stood up, picked up the shovels and went to it again.

Many years later my brother wrote a book about some of this which he entitled "Whatever It Takes". This was certainly the partnership policy.

One night we were camping adjacent to a water hole, and I went to the water about ten meters away to fill the billy can. A few steps into returning I debated whether to step over a stick about eight feet long. I decided in the negative, and as I avoided the stick it moved off. Next morning, I tracked the snake into the exposed base of a tree hollow.

This was the habitat of inland taipans which grow to these lengths, possess, incontestably, the most deadly venom known to man, and have a hypodermic injection system too. After this I became more sensitive to sleeping on the ground amongst them. They are known to be attracted to one's body warmth, and then cuddle up to it. After this I continued to sleep on the ground for the full three months but had increasing doubts and some dreams about it.

Later, when sleeping out drilling in another location on top of the Great Dividing Range, I had invested in a camp stretcher. While the next morning was a warm one, I awoke absolutely freezing. An amazingly heavy dew had my blankets completely sopping wet. I learned of the need for an impervious cover in heavy dews.

The day came when I was building our pole house. By this time, I had degenerated into sophistication. The site was then just building materials stacked about. I even had a foam rubber mattress, so it went on top of a stack of timber. Dreams of snakes joining me still revisited me occasionally. With a blanket or two I was all set, but it was a humid night and a heavy dew might be expected. What to do? I grabbed a sheet of galvanised iron, pulled it over me and slept very well. This is how one of the favourite stories my friends like to tell about me came to be spread far and wide.

A dear friend, very urbane, came unexpectedly the next morning to visit me. He looked about and I wasn't there. Then the unthinkable happened. A sheet of iron began to move up and aside, and I emerged from under it. He told this story for the rest of his life. To his mind, he had witnessed the greatest testimony to bush innovation. "He was sleeping under a sheet of galvanised iron" he said, and thought it an inconceivable adaptation to bedroom comfort, and beyond the wildest bounds of any imagined or definable luxury. To me it was just a matter of whatever it takes.

In a heavy wind a loose sheet of iron can slice a man in two. But I knew I was safe, because no matter the direction of such a wind, it would always carry it away from me.

The "dream" happened later. The poles were up, and the roof of the two-story structure was on. My truck was parked under it, and I had a mattress and blankets on its deck. I was sleeping completely under a sheet of canvas this time, to defeat the mosquitoes. It was a warm night and very dark under the thick canvas. Then it happened. This time it was not a dream: a snake was slowly crawling over my chest.

On such occasions, panic is completely out of the question. I disciplined myself to await his passing, which happened slowly. Best not risk any precipitate action from him. When I adjudged him likely out of range, I violently threw back the canvas and flung my legs over the edge of the truck, looking about in the morning light. There was no snake. Another bloody snake dream! The most realistic one I had ever had. How bloody silly of me!

As I sat there in my foolishness, I was facing my station wagon about eight meters away. Although I was relaxed by now, there was something unusual about it. There was a light-coloured perimeter encircling my black front tyre. Then I knew what it was. There was a completely placid non-venomous green tree snake lying over the black rubber.

What was real became a dream. Then the dream became an enigmatic mystery beyond discernment. Could that which seemed so real, which then dissolved into a bad dream, and then produced a witness as testimony of its reality, ever produce a verdict? Was it real or a dream?

Though now thirty years ago, the jury is still out.

Whilst I am tempted to draw an analogy or two here, it is a little too close to home. The relationship between the mind and things is the sole determinant of sanity. In this case I am indeterminately placed where the real and the mental conception are indiscernible, so my madness is, perhaps, an open question. I will pass on the analogies.

You are free to hypothesise any from your own experiences, as you will.

In terms of well-known Australian colloquialisms, may I bask in the affectionate categorisation of my peers as a "silly poor bastard"?

EXTRANEOUS EXCEPTIONALLY EXASPERATING EXACTITUDES

A title such as the above is a sure sign that the author is going to launch forth in unrelated, uncoordinated, and possibly incomprehensible prose. When one has a number of ingredients which cannot be baked into any recognisable dish, the thing is to boldly set them upon the table with some euphemism for leftovers, such as the above.

The first inanity with which I would like to take issue, is that the rule to drive on the right side of the road is the equal of driving on the left. With obedience, each is said to be the other's equal. Alas, right and wrong even enter into the question of right or left.

It has long been observed that when people enter a supermarket, they usually circulate in a clockwise direction. There is usually some essential on the extreme right of the entrance at the back, to ensure that shoppers go the full circuit. Temptation is thus in their path a little longer. Why do people circulate like this?

Because most are right-handed. In circulating clockwise their sword arm is facing any possible encounter, while their left is protected by the wall. Are people really more aware and conscious of things on their right side? Yes, and we know it. Why else would we describe unexpected surprises as "coming out of left field"?

In driving on the right side, the greatest threat comes on your least conscious, and least able side, the left. Of course, changing to the safest side would take a generation. In this time, as it was in Australia during World War II when the locals were regularly killed on the crest of hills by Americans on "the wrong side", carnage would reign.

Thus, it is possibly best, if you can spare them, to sacrifice a few extra people each year, rather than take many more casualties in the short term to correct the historical mistake.

To show that I can be even more contentious than this, let's talk climate. Professor Michel van Biezen is evangelistic about science. He has more than a hundred videos about physics on his YouTube channel. His video presentations on CO^2 as a greenhouse gas are seemingly from another era. He presents his material as though nothing is relevant in science other than whether it is true or not. He seems oblivious to the well laid theses of fear which everywhere compete for the grant monies of the intimidated.

He blithely points out that while the heat (infrared radiation) escaping from earth back into space has wavelengths from about 0.6 to 20 microns, CO^2 is completely impotent except at two small apertures. It can only operate at all in the vicinity of radiation of wavelengths of 4.27 microns, and those between 14 and 16 microns. So as an absolute maximum, CO^2 only has access to 18% of the infrared radiation escaping earth.

Water vapour is the most effective greenhouse gas, however, and it also operates at these same wavelengths. For every CO^2 molecule in the atmosphere, there are twenty molecules of water vapour, and they do most of the work of warming the atmosphere. So what is left after water vapour has grabbed its lot of heat escaping into space? 4 to 4.5% is all that is available for CO^2 to intercept, and of this it has now already captured perhaps more than 90%.

It is all a great disappointment to those creating consternation at a threatening climate. If you view his video https://www.youtube.com/watch?v=o8n vdDXR8ZE more similar and associated ones will also be offered to you. He does not avoid secondary questions such as the rate of slowing the progress of heat escaping earth, either. The video link displaying this also disappoints. https://www.youtube.com/watch?v=GAv-ZwjCwss

Normally, anyone divulging incongruous "exactitudes" such as the above will offer suggestions as to their moral, social, physical, or other implications. This may be counterproductive. If society is to make sense of its situation, it will need the efforts of all people. All hands will be needed at the pumps, and all minds at puzzling the public quantum of ponderous allegations. The reader will need to do this for himself; discerning truth is the most important (and interesting) social function given to us. Everyone playing Sherlock Holmes at unearthing public deception in communications, comes to enjoy it as the greatest game offering.

All conforming to the views most commonly propounded, if it be on the basis that inquiry disturbs comfort, are committing intellectual suicide. So, what does it mean in its widest implications if CO^2 is incapable of significant or threatening climate disturbance? Yes, the world is depending upon your answer, and it is all up to you, so it may be worth an effort.

It is probably true that asking any person to think about more than three difficult things in one day is an act of considerable, if not outright cruelty. For this reason, though the world abounds in imponderables, I will only venture one further for today.

The question is "Do exceptions prove the rule?" Does, for instance, the fact that the Twin Towers and also Building Seven fell down in a manner never before observed except in cases of professional demolition, prove that they were not demolished, and therefore were exceptions? And if so, what rule were they proving?

The lower structures of these buildings had supported the full weight above them for decades and had not been affected by the 'plane crashes. Then, seemingly in an instant, their resistance to gravity so diminished that each building fell at freefall acceleration. In one moment, all was supported, and in the next, no resistance to gravity at all was evident.

I know of course that this happened in America, and I have heard of something in which Americans apparently believe called "American Exceptionalism".

But can this possibly explain what happened on the eleventh day of the ninth month?

THE RETURN OF A KING?

T he recent death of Queen Elizabeth II brought forth a profusion of accolades for her long life of service. Large crowds assembled and the world watched the events which followed. This all evidenced the mystical attractive power of monarchy which establishes the zenith of political power as an overt and personal responsibility.

The reassurance of monarchy is that a known and acknowledged person stands above all the conniving politicians, their lobbyists, and their army of urgers. In the final analysis a liege lord beloved by his/her subjects can trump any chicanery, and politics plays no part in the monarch's ascent to power. Monarchy curbs all committees with a penultimate "committee of one".

The importance of the above should suffer no detraction, and certainly none is intended, but sometimes things have to be said to jolt us into our senses.

The reign of Queen Elizabeth II from 1953 to 2022 was the most disappointing in terms of lost opportunities in the history of the British peoples. How can that be?

At the coronation of 1953 there was the prospect of a real British Commonwealth; a confederation of independent nations acting in cooperation to bring a significant force into the world offering Western values, responsible freedoms, and stability to its peoples and to the world at large.

Geographically the United Kingdom, Canada, Australia, and New Zealand would have been represented on both sides of the North Atlantic Ocean, in both the North and South Pacific, and on the East of the Indian Ocean.

In mineral resources these nations have it all. Their peoples are intelligent and highly educated with a common heritage well disposing them to cooperative action and good sense in world affairs; a "Third Force" or at least a significant force for stability and peace.

In 1953 these nations had a Preferential Trade Agreement with each other which was not destroyed until the then Queen signed into being the Act which took the United Kingdom into the debacle of the European Common Market. Would not a Crown Commonwealth of Nations have grown increasingly in shared economic prosperity without this intervention?

A British Commonwealth of Nations which shared a Crown, and a common heritage and culture was left stillborn in the womb in the worship of "political correctness". Why?

Because such dissimilar and unsuitable nations for a real Commonwealth, such as Pakistan and Uganda, for example, could not be told to go away.

It is not yet too late for these four nations to form a confederation of power, resources, and influence equal to that of the United States, but a beginning can only be made by clearly recognising that the present commonwealth is a farce - and then by developing economic, defence, and other relationships between the legitimate children of British heritage. Do we now have a Monarch who will not throw a tantrum at the thought of a pruned and reinvigorated real Crown Commonwealth being brought into being?

RABBITS AND A TIGER

BY TOBY MALONEY

Many years ago I met a jolly and good natured fellow, and this despite his physical disabilities. He was good humoured and he also had an almost encyclopaedic memory, so he could quote you many wise and interesting things that had been said through the ages.

A more plausible and likeable fellow I have never met. I loved him dearly.

He came, I suppose, to believe that well known conception of the honest woodman: that you can fool all the people some of the time, some all the time, but not all for all the time. As a result he resolved to seek out from the folk around him what they thought, for he knew that they were not wrong, at least, not all the time.

So every Sunday, this almost religious tenet drove him into the market places. Here he asked important questions and noted the answers of all that would hesitate long enough to endure him.

Many such types who run questionnaires, or act as highly moral journalists in the service of our ever-vigilant media, have a normal line of questioning which runs to penetrating questions such as "Is it true that you murdered your Grandmother last week with a club for three shillings and sixpence?" If you say "No" the immediate rejoinder is "Then you deny that you murdered your Grandmother last week with a club for three shillings and sixpence do you?"

My friend, of course, would never have asked such questions.

However he was given at times to posing bland and hypothetical conundrums such as, for instance:

1. Do you think money grows on trees?

2. Do you sometimes suspect that some human agency may be creating it?

3. As the money supply increased by 10% last year, how is this possible if all means of creating it out of nothing are illegal?

4. If government creates any of it, why is it never listed as revenue in the Treasury's Annual Budgets?

This sort of nonsense is of course completely reprehensible, and ought never to be asked, let alone answered. Yet somehow in spite of his appalling bad taste, one was tempted to forgive him.

Of course, Sunday after Sunday, he asked thousands upon thousands of questions about immigration, import duties, taxation, criminal law and the constitution. However, the ones which drew the most profound interest that he ever raised were (1) Do you like peanut butter sandwiches? (2) Would your dog bite if sufficiently provoked? & (3) Why did the Voter cross the road?

Now all this polling of "the will of the body politic" brought him to a high fervour. Poor Yorick! To him, if the prevailing view of 51% was that tomatoes should be taxed at 1.37%, it was as good as enshrined in legislation before sundown - that's democracy, he'd say.

He'd lived in a democracy all his life, he would declare, and he planned to die in one also, unless a better idea came along which he would immediately reject, of course, as impossible.

So he would collate the results of his consultations with public opinion, and hurry them off to the government, knowing that what the people think is eagerly anticipated and acted upon with resolution and expedition.

Now one day a gentleman with every appearance of respectability and sanity came to our Yorick and asked questions of him, instead. Firstly he asked:

"If it is possible for a Tiger to whisper into the ear of one politician, do you suppose it might be possible for him to also whisper into the ear of another?"

"I suppose it might," said Yorick.

"Now if it were possible for a Tiger to make lots of money- ("You mean earn lots?" interjected Yorick. "No I mean *make*" replied the gentleman) "do you suppose that he may ladle a little into any ear into which he whispered?"

"He could with the right funnel," said Yorick.

"Now while the Tiger is whispering into one ear, do you suppose that with enough money and thought, he might hire perhaps 27 others to whisper many disparate and conflicting notions simultaneously into the other?"

"He could," said Yorick.

And may he perfume the air about him, and safely leave it to the clever people to smell the advantage of closely associating with the Tiger?

"Absolutely," said Yorick.

"Well then," said the gentleman, "I admire your efforts towards democracy, and would like to assist you to see how effective you can really be. By answering just two questions, you can grow in this important wisdom. Will you do it?"

"Of course," said Yorick.

"Then what say ye my good Yorick to these:

"How many rabbits does it take to kill a Tiger, or defeat him in combat?

"And secondly, what percentage of rabbits show a propensity to attack tigers?"

Surely there could not be more to politics than democratic ideals?

With the above thoughts in mind, we might consider the case of a tiger called Arabella. This tiger lives in the US and in 2020 spent $1.2 billion on "social causes". It funds and is funded by a mixture of entities. These include the Sixteen Thirty Fund, the New Venture Fund, the Hopewell Fund, Good Information, and the North Fund. Their social causes include supporting gun control, amnesty for illegal immigrants, fossil fuel bans, legalising marijuana, relaxing voting laws, taxpayer funded abortion and other noble efforts.[1]

While this tiger is known to be largely fed by George Soros, other donors include Hansjorg Wyss, Reid Hoffman and of course, the Bill and Melinda Gates Foundation which has given $250 million since 2009. Their donations can remain anonymous if they wish.

Those in the rabbit class, however, not having tax free foundations and sophisticated legal structures, can't give more than $200 to a political party without their donations being recorded and published.

To rephrase the conundrum, how many openly given donations of $200 does it take to outdo $1.2 billion given anonymously? Six million is the answer, though the next question is "Can six million be found who will throw $200 each at a tiger?" And a further important consideration is that Arabella obviously knows her way around the top end of town, rather better than do six million amateur (if not witless) rabbits.

The tiger has to be seen as the odds-on favourite thus far. Because the animal which can create all money costlessly, own it, and employ it at will, has won all rounds hitherto. And furthermore, the propensity of six million rabbits to come hopping over the hill with malicious intent towards tigers, is yet to be observed.

Still, with the truth all things are possible, and perhaps the six million are just on the other side of the horizon?

---

1. https://www.youtube.com/watch?v=DDfaZcNi8lQ An expose of Arabella.

THE USE OF COMMON SENSE

BY TOBY MALONEY, 2016

C ould it be that best language practice involves conveying clarity of meaning with economy?

If so, what is it that the words "utilise" and "utilisation" convey that the word "use" does not? Why is "utilised" used at all? Its purpose would seem to be wholly in imparting an impression of one's erudition to an audience. Those interested in giving this impression may find the suggestions below helpful in its reinforcement.

Once the word "utilise" is granted legitimacy, then "utilisation" (the use of) must be granted as a valid word, as also must "utilisation**alistic**" (much given to the use of things). Those who practice the use of many things in different activities such as transportation, nutrition or entertainment are of course "**multi**utilisation**alistic**", or as one may say, much given over to "multi**utilisation**alistic**ism**".

Of course those who misuse things in many areas, and those who oppose them, are respectively "**mis**multi**utilisation**alistic**ismists**" and "**anti**mis**multi**utilisation**alistic**ismists**". Those who would not quite describe themselves in this way, but who are sympathetic nevertheless, are of course known as "**Neo**anti**mis**multi**utilisation**alistic**ismists**". Even if you hold me to be in error in this thing, you must surely allow that I am a misutilisationalisticismist, at the very least.

Considering that George Bernard Shaw worked up his longest word in the English language from the "establishment" of the Church of England, to give us the word "antidisestablishmentarianism" of 28 letters, and we have started from the handicap of the three letter word "use", the erudition of the human race has clearly taken a quantum leap forward, for those who are ambivalent about opposing multiple misuses; the "**Neo**anti**mis**multi**utilisation**alistic**ismists**" have a moniker of 40 letters, no less.

To paraphrase Marx, "Neoantimismultiutilisationalisticismists of the world unite, you have nothing to lose (or should it have been "use") but your brains!"

TRAINING MONKEYS AND OTHERS

You start with a cage containing four monkeys, and inside the cage you hang a banana on a string, and then you place a set of stairs under the banana. Before long a monkey will go to the stairs and climb toward the banana. You then spray ALL the monkeys with cold water. After a while, another monkey makes an attempt. As soon as he touches the stairs, you spray ALL the monkeys with cold water again. Pretty soon, when another monkey tries to climb the stairs, the other monkeys will try to prevent it.

Now, put away the cold water. Remove one monkey from the cage and replace it with a new monkey. The new monkey sees the banana and attempts to climb the stairs. To his shock, ALL of the other monkeys beat the stuffing out of him. After another attempt and attack, he knows that if he tries to climb the stairs he will be assaulted.

Next, remove another of the original four monkeys, replacing it with a new monkey. The newcomer goes to the stairs and is attacked. The previous newcomer takes part in the punishment with enthusiasm - because he is now part of the "team." Then, replace a third original monkey with a new monkey, followed by a fourth. Every time the newest monkey takes to the stairs, he is attacked.

Now, the monkeys who are beating him up have no idea why they were not permitted to climb the stairs. Neither do they know why they are participating in the beating of the newest monkey. Having replaced all of the original monkeys, none of the remaining monkeys will have ever been sprayed with cold water. Nevertheless, not one of the monkeys will try to climb the stairway for the banana. Why, you ask?

Because in their minds, that is the way it has always been!

This is how today's House and Senate in Australia operates, and this is why, from time to time,

ALL of the monkeys need to be REPLACED AT THE SAME TIME!

Put All Sitting Members Last!

See chapter entitled *If You Really Have Had Enough,* page 113, for a fuller explanation of the best technique for training politicians.

Disclaimer: This is meant with no disrespect to monkeys.

THE PROBLEM OF GROVELMENT

Although politicians in Australia have been universally held in low regard as a class throughout our history, several unexamined factors have perhaps militated against the full measure of their deserved contempt being publically realised and appreciated.

The purpose of this article is to examine this proposition to at least some preliminary degree.

Perhaps the greatest factor in the politician's defence is derived from an Australian sense of fair play. This instinct unconsciously insists, quite correctly, that any body of persons chosen largely at random from amongst us, simply could not be as consistently bad as the evidence from every quarter and angle, both loudly and seemingly incontrovertibly, insists.

No Australian of voting age has not on numerous occasions pondered, in association with his peers, this mysterious phenomenon. On all occasions to which I have been a party, all explanations put forward, however aggressively, passionately or even provisionally, have met with a consensus of tentative agreement. This is true of both main theses; the dismissive "*They are all a pack of b......s*" and the more philosophical observations such as "*All power tends to corrupt*".

While agreed that the performance of politicians, irrespective of parties, has been one of willful and vindictive misrepresentation against the electorate on a great many important issues, this almost universal consensus has remained tentative. Tentative, because although their record of misrepresentation on myriad issues is incontrovertible, credulity at the depth and number of perfidious politicians is seriously strained when contemplated as a burgeoning social phenomenon.

Far from lamenting this faltering credulity it should be seen in some measure as fortuitous. A final rather than a tentative acceptance of this judgement, though all the known facts would seem to support it, would have brought down upon political practitioners the verdict of "guilty of misrepresentation with extreme prejudice", and this would have placed the whole of national democratic life at considerable risk.

Subsequent to such a verdict present structures would have most certainly been torn down in outrage, with the one essential understanding necessary for constructive correction, namely an appreciation of the underlying cause of political delinquency, by its absence, precluding a remedial democratic outcome.

Acceptance of the full measure of politicians' iniquity has been held back from total adoption with its inevitable resulting action, with an attitude which speculated that "surely, they just couldn't be that bad!" This implies a suspicion that somehow "We must have gotten it wrong".

The key to the growing revulsion at all political parties is the slowly emerging realisation that politicians, no matter which party they represent, are not, *definitely not,* the result of a selection based on virtue, nor on a random process either.

All electors will understand that if one went through the prisons and selected a group of persons guilty of certain particular crimes, their group activity would be predetermined. Similarly, if one assembled from the population those who had given the greatest unrewarded and selfless service in public life, different personal characteristics would be evident in such a group.

The political parties act as filters through which only persons of a particular type may ascend.

The requirements for success in political parties are the personal characteristics found in increasing purity as one ascends through the various levels of the party structure, and reaches its zenith in parliamentary representatives.

What are these personal characteristics?

They are defined by the innate nature of Parties. The formula for succeeding in political parties is a simple one. *The Formula* is as follows:-

1. Select a party.

2. Join it.

3. Discern who it is that exercises the real power in that party.

4. Make yourself available as an agent of these persons' influence. Do this with the utmost dedication and application, bringing to bear all of your personal abilities and talents, intelligence and initiative in their service. There are others competing with you in prostrating servitude, so submissive effort is essential to your advancement.

5. Learn through your experience in both the defeats and victories of your service to the influence for these powerful others, to submerge your independence of mind and inclination whilst at the same time drawing a veil over your motives couched in terms of the highest moral considerations at your command.

6. In this way the party's powerful are recruited into promoting yourself. You will need to accept whatever increases in responsibility and position which the interests of the powerful dictate for you, and are for their reasons offered.

7. Remember always that there are plenty of others in your party who instinctively understand this formula, and that the extent to which they do is the accurate measure of their intended threat to yourself.

8. Never forget that this competition is decided absolutely upon performance. Your record of delivery in accordance with the will of the

party's powerful alone, is your only worthwhile political capital.

Essential Accompanying Ignorances

1. That after the mean average incubation period for politicians of approximately 10 to 20 years before election, plus further years as a junior backbencher and then as a junior cabinet minister, the necessary modus operandi of conforming to the formula as it impacts upon your personality, and the social expectations of all those around you, will preclude any exercise of creative independent integrity. You will not have developed any.

2. That for this reason your original good intentions, to first acquire power, and then use it for good, will in no circumstances be achievable, nor indeed be remembered by yourself.

3. That your net political contribution to posterity will be to preclude those, who through maintenance of a creative independent integrity, will have long since sickened of the party political process and gone home. The one personal quality which your country absolutely needs for its wellbeing is the very one you will have positively denied it. It is enough.

This is the problem of Grovelment in Government.

Nursing Gunpowder

Suppose you had an enemy who was seeking to steal your girlfriend, blacken your reputation and ruin your property. What would you do if you accidentally discovered that he was planning to commit a serious crime? There are three likely options.

A few would run to him bragging that he had been discovered, whereupon he could save himself from the ignominy of being caught and punished, and then return to his designs upon you.

The majority, being those who don't do thinking, but outsource it to others, would share this knowledge with sundry persons and consult them upon advised action. In this way the ripples of this information would spread, control of its use would be lost, and its benefit might accrue anywhere.

Another rarer class of persons would nurse it, hold it close and observe the crime in preparation, and in process of accomplishment. They would wait until the culpability of the enemy was obvious upon exposure, and only then would the authorities be informed. This is the high art in secret intelligence operations.

A classic case of this was with Mary Queen of Scots. Her firebrand supporters found a means of communicating with her during her incarceration by Queen Elizabeth I. They advised her of their coming intent to free her and received responses. This was organised through the fellow who was responsible for supplying her material needs in captivity. His actual loyalty was to the Government authorities.

The messages back and forth were copied, but otherwise delivered. The conspiracy was nursed with William Cecil (1st Baron Burghley) playing the role of mastermind until the attempted rescue was made. Then the gallants of the rescue all lost their lives, but they were never the object. Queen Mary was implicated, and her execution was then justified, or at least politically enabled in 1587. Nursing offered and delivered the complete route of the adventurers' intents. The fact of nursing in this case is not contested.

The execution of the Catholic mother at an age of 45 years, eliminated her from succession, and brought her Protestant son James 1st to the throne of England 16 years later in 1603. In 1605 a most dramatic attempt was made to blow up Parliament with 36 barrels of gunpowder.

The conspirators were Catholic. Guy Fawkes was caught in the act. His fellow conspirators were either taken or killed in the taking. Catholicism was painted as anti-patriotic, and the reformation was at last secure in England.

Most commentators concentrate their comment on the Protestant/Catholic theological conflagration. I will not.

Four centuries after the event, conclusions are not to be had; but my interest is in examining the case for the nursing of the so-called "gunpowder plot".

Firstly, there is the matter of the source of all this gunpowder. Its manufacture was said to be a government monopoly at the time. The real instigator and leader of the plot was Robert Catesby, and he asked Ambrose Rookwood to acquire the gunpowder. He did so under the pretext of supplying it for the use of the English Regiment in Flanders, which was in the service of Spain, which was in an English alliance at that time.

The powder mills were at various sites, many of which were around London, including Rotherhithe, Long Ditton in Surrey, Leigh Place near Godstone, and Faversham. The regulation of sales was not particularly tight, it seems, but nevertheless it raises a question. Was the intelligence service run by Robert Cecil, extremely efficient in many respects, without a watching brief on this important commodity of insurrection? A careful watch was kept upon the recusants, as the resisting Catholics were known, yet was their acquisition of about 2,000 pounds of gunpowder unobserved?

Certainly, one would think it would have been stopped once observed. But there is another twist. Gunpowder in time is known to "decay", as it was said, when its components, sulphur, charcoal, and saltpetre separate. To reconstitute it alcohol and water were added, it was oven dried, and its components broken into small crumbs to make "corned-powder", the reactivated form. Decayed gunpowder would not explode.

After the discovery of the plot on the 5th of November, the gunpowder was removed to "His Majesty's store within the office of Ordnance" in the Tower of London on the 7th. The powder was officially described as "decayed". As it turned out, the only danger of the powder was in the incrimination of the plotters.

Is this fortuitous state of the powder evidence of Robert Cecil's intelligence network being aware of, and nursing the plot from an early stage? Was the gunpowder decayed, or close to decaying at its acquisition? If so, could the plot be allowed to "ripen" until a most dramatic and late stage of the intended crime was arrived at, and this without risk?

Had Cecil foreknowledge of the plot from an early stage, this would present him with a problem in its later stages. If he admitted to this, his failure to end the threat earlier would be damnable, though had he exposed the threat earlier, the dramatic late exposure of an imminent danger and the revulsion at the heinous threat posed by criminal Catholics would be lessened. The conviction that Catholicism was unpatriotic, criminal, treasonous and violent could not have been burned so deeply into English consciousness for the next hundred years and more. How would this dilemma of non-exposure, if it existed, have been solved?

Exposure came in the form of an anonymous letter. Even with the capture and torture of the culprits, its origin was never discovered. The letter was delivered anonymously to a servant of Lord Monteagle on the 26th of October. Monteagle was known to have Catholic sympathies but was unlikely to concur in or conceal so mysterious a threat and warning. He didn't. He took it to Robert Cecil whom he knew and was not far distant. It read:

My Lord, out of the love I bear to some of your friends, I have a care of your preservation. Therefore I would advise you, as you tender your life, to devise some excuse to shift of your attendance at this Parliament; for God and man hath concurred to punish the wickedness of this time. And think not slightly of this advertisement, but retire yourself to your country (county) where you may expect the event in safety. For though there is no appearance of any stir, yet I say they shall receive a terrible blow this Parliament; and yet they will not see who hurts them. This counsel is not to be condemned because it may do you good and can do you no harm; for the danger is passed as soon as you have burned the letter. And I hope God will give you the grace to make good use of it, to whose holy protection I commend you.

Cecil took the letter to King James himself once he returned from his hunting in Cambridgeshire five days later on the 31st, though he had told members of the Council including the Catholic Lord Worcester and Lord Northampton of it. The delay in informing the King may be thought to be of significance given its gravity. Cecil apparently thought he had time to deal with it.

From the King's own account of his being informed of the letter, published in his book *King's History,* Cecil said that the letter must have been written "by a fool" and drew the King's attention to the phrase "the danger is past as soon as you have burnt the letter", which he said he found quite meaningless. The King responded that he thought "powder" was being suggested. In this way it was the King himself who discerned the nature of the threat. Well done Cecil, or more properly, Lord Salisbury as he had become.

Cecil was content to wait for his master's return, which he later casually explained by saying that waiting would afford more time for the plot "to ripen". Unless he was already privy to the facts, why such confidence that he was in command of the situation? It is true that the opening of Parliament, the likely time of the planned event with the King present, was still five days off, but until the King's assertion that he thought "powder" was involved, Cecil hadn't mentioned the word.

It is known that Fawkes' name had already been entered into Cecil's files well before his capture.

On Saturday the 2nd the Council resolved to take some action on the threat to Parliament previously revealed to them by Cecil. It was decided that the Lord Chamberlain, Lord Suffolk, should "view" the Parliament "both above and below". Yet the search did not take place until Monday the 4th, the day before Parliament was to meet. This delay is explained in the *King's History* on page 199, as partly because it would be best to make the search "the nearer that things were to readiness".

The official report mentions two searches, so apparently the first failed. Cecil's first report to the English ambassadors abroad mentions only one search, and that around midnight. The gunpowder was discovered behind a large amount of firewood in a cellar.

Around midnight or perhaps in the early hours of the 5th of November, a figure in a cloak and dark hat was discovered skulking beneath the precincts of Parliament and was immediately apprehended. This was Guy Fawkes, and though really a minion in the conspiracy, it has been forever attributed to him rather than its true instigator, Robert Catesby, who was killed in the attempt to capture him.

There was never any need for Cecil to invent the plot's desperadoes; there is ever enough of those whose political simplicity cannot comprehend the danger of their endeavours misfiring. And moreover, without a suspicion of an intelligence service and leadership of the genius of a Cecil, they are ever-ready meat to the wiles of such.

Cecil didn't (and didn't need to) invent any plotters in the persecution and vilification of Catholicism; they came to him as manna from heaven. Did he, however, nurse them? Did he watch their endeavours ripen? Did he see to it that their acquired gunpowder was decayed? No revelation was ever made by the investigators as to which manufacturers supplied the powder. The torturers apparently didn't ask. Could this have been because it would have led honest inquiry toward speaking to the staff and management of these powder mills? A knowledge of Government scrutiny could have been had there.

The negligence of scrutiny of gunpowder purchases by a man like Cecil, when even the slowest intellect would think it a necessary routine of intelligence gathering, is surely suggestive of an intent not to admit that such was diligently done?

At four hundred years' distance, when the evidence was always the property of a most able intelligence service anyhow, it is not going to offer any proof of "nursing". But it has to be asked by us all: when does an abundance of probability result in a verdict of "Probably guilty of nursing as charged?"

Cecil's triumph was remarkable and long lasting. Catholics could not receive a university degree nor vote in local elections until 1707; 192 years hence. They were not permitted to vote in Parliamentary elections until the Catholic Emancipation (Act) of 1829, 224 years after the gunpowder plot of 1605.

Some suspect that the lessons learned by "nursing gunpowder" have continued to be employed through "intelligence negligence". Indignant reprisal enabling public support for war is most readily accomplished by nursing psychopaths.

This essay has been written from the research of Antonia Fraser in her work *The Gunpowder Plot*, first published in the UK by Weidenfeld and Nicolson in 1996.

NIL SINE LABORE

In my early teens I attended a school of some antiquity which was very proud of its academic record. Some 150 years previously its founders had proclaimed its motto as *Nil Sine Labore*. While this translates as "Nothing Without Labour", whenever we students were asked for the school's motto we would always give it as "No Sign of Labour".

While it is not to be borne that a small boy in short pants would berate and ridicule his school's motto, and jump on its flowers, as it were, perhaps one may eventually ask when the statute of limitations expires in such cases. These sixty years I have held my peace at this ridiculous, false, and even dangerous motto. Today I become the first Old Boy to break his silence, and perhaps my name will be blackened forever for proffering the obvious.

A couple of questions will expose the nonsense. Does sunshine exist? If so, what labour has been invested in its production? Unless sunshine is indeed nothing, then the school motto is rubbish.

Perhaps the founders sought to encourage the students towards effort, but I suspect that this was more the ostensible rather than the operative motive. Man has always enjoyed looking at such as the pyramids, city skylines, or the Panama Canal, and saying "I did this. We did this. Man did this."

Are my fellow Old Boys then to look at rainbows, the moon, or the Himalayan mountains and say to themselves "We did this"? Those who attended Brisbane Grammar School are indubitably obliged to think so.

OK, so the motto is stupid and false, but I said it is also dangerous. Indeed, it is. Why? Because it ascribes to labour a distorted and exaggerated place in the human economy, which, whatever its place in the past, is atrophying in its input to production with every advance in technology and automated process.

Let us juxtapose the input of labour against that of our industrial inheritance in building a house. Using the products of our industrial knowledge such as steel saws and chisels, and the myriad power tools and means of affixing now in use, it takes X man-days to build a house. Take away not only the tools, but the concepts and knowhow of metallurgy and methodology received from our forebears also, and we could not build houses at all. A few leaves thrown over some leaning sticks would be about the extent of it. Caves would be our only recourse.

The role of labour in production has been declining through history. As this advances the rules of distribution will have to be adjusted. The rules once said (or were said to have said) that "Labour produces all wealth", and that "He who would not work, neither shall he eat". So, if we arrive in a world in which one hundred persons can produce all the material necessities (and desirables too) of life for a thousand persons, do we amend the social arrangements? Nine hundred shall not be allowed to eat then, because they did not work?

The main means of production is now our industrial inheritance, and for this reason, there is no alternative but to have its distribution henceforth, also based upon inheritance. "He who will not work will be paid a National Dividend on the basis of his industrial inheritance" will invoke a storm of anguished moral indignation and protest from all who are cultured in the past of scarcity.

What shall we give those who, by the historic efforts of their forebears, have seen work (the curse of Adam) lifted from their backs and placed upon machines? Perhaps in keeping with our school motto we should give them whatever, but give it as debt, thereby insisting that it be returned and repaid.

To give as a debt is to give nothing, and then perhaps it is all right? That will distribute what is due from our inheritance, but we will have to repay it, and then have it loaned out to us again, enmeshing us forever in a minefield of enumerated abstractions in cyberspace, otherwise commonly known as money, or more properly as debt-money.

The difficult thing for us Old Boys to get our heads around, is understanding the prefix to numbers. The number one may be expressed in two forms, that is -1 or +1. Money also comes in these alternate forms of -$1 and +$1.

Whenever we produced more in consumer goods than the amount which we were paid to do so, our incomes were insufficient to buy all that we had produced. We could not buy that part of our production which was our profit; the increment over and above what the inducement for us to produce it had cost. Unless sufficient funds were had to clear industry's production, the economy would go into recession. The thing to do was debt (for we can't allow something for nothing) and so in time the aggregate of all of our former profits formed up and constituted our national debt. It grows every year in every country.

Having shaken off the mesmerism of our motto may I moot an idea of monetary moment? If the needed extra funds were distributed as a "plus figure" instead of a minus one, the national debt would atrophy. When a positive meets a negative, it is like matter meeting antimatter: 'p*hffif*#', and there is nothing there at all.

We Grammarians will have to amend our precepts somewhat if the meek are to inherit the earth. *Labore Sine Nil* - labour without nothing - will be necessary to 'empay' those whose inheritance of previous efforts have provisioned them.

The choice is simple enough. We may become the proprietors of our inheritance, or alternately, proletariats increasingly without function.

Proprietors of the world unite, for there is nothing to be lost other than your paid jobs. In paid leisure, your service to others will increasingly be of your own choosing; the service of which Saint Augustine of Hippo once wrote: "that service in which is perfect freedom".

THE PROSTITUTE CALLED SCIENCE

What is a scientist?

"A scientist is a person who makes up scary stories in order to frighten the body politic into giving his organisation grants to fund research."

This statement is scandalous, defamatory, and outrageous. Yes, that is so, and it is also true perhaps 50% of the time.

For science to be accepted it has to be demonstrable, and most importantly, repeatedly demonstrable. If a scientific paper claims that when certain substances are placed in certain relationships, circumstances, and conditions, a specified result will be observed, that is not science. It becomes science only when it is confirmed by repeated experimentation. Science which is not repeatable is not science. It may be storytelling, mythology, an active imagination, wishful thinking, a zealousness to do good, or fraud or something else again. The only surety is what it is not; it is not science.

Gaining increasing attention in science now is what is called the "replication crisis". Professor John Ioannidis of Stanford University impelled it into wider discussion with his published paper of 2005 entitled "Why Most Published Research Findings Are False." In it he stated:

"There is increasing concern that in modern research, false findings may be the majority or even the vast majority of published research claims. However, this should not be surprising. It can be proven that most claimed research findings are false."

An article in *Nature Review Drug Discovery* in 2011 by scientists from the drug company Bayer, claimed that 75% of the literature used for potential drug discovery targets is not reliable. As the magazine *The Economist* of 19/10/2013 said: "A rule of thumb among biotechnology venture-capitalists is that half of published research cannot be replicated. Last year researchers at one biotech firm, Amgen, found they could reproduce just six of 53 "landmark" studies in cancer research."

Surely this was not wholly a matter of fabricating evidence. Some error would be from incompetence no doubt, and some would be arrived at through an un-acknowledged wish to please with a politically acceptable or popular outcome. One would need a well-developed ability to delude numbers of people in one's team to arrive at unreplicable nonsense so often. One suspects the possibility of a future Nobel Prize being awarded for contributing to our understanding of "Why bullshit baffles brains?".

Peter Ridd, a marine geophysicist formerly of James Cook University, in his recent book *Reef Heresy* examines the claims that human activity has damaged the Great Barrier Reef through: nutrient pollution from agriculture causing the crown-of-thorns starfish to multiply, dredging shipping lanes, climate change, coal dust, overfishing and herbicides. Not one of these claims has been able to be verified to any significant, or even measurable degree.[1]

Hundreds of millions of dollars have been spent on "saving the reef"; the world is convinced that the reef is dead or dying, and all this is based on science which is not replicable. The producers of alarmists' "scientific" papers have been well rewarded indeed for their duplicitous propagandising. Though few would ever dare to say so, the whole of marine science on this issue takes on a distinctly brothel-like hue. I say this in the hope that it will be proved to be so,

---

1. Peter Ridd's work of 278 pages 'Reef Heresy', published by Connor Court Publishing Pty Ltd in 2020 is available from sales@connorcourt.com

that a good verbal thrashing can produce discipline and reform, and that this proves to be a replicable science.

Would that it were true that these instances of the sciences' self-abasement are isolated. Alas, it would appear not. The alarmism over CO2 presents another prime suspect of a scary story designed to loosen up the cash boxes of the frightened.

Carbon dioxide is known by true science to be both an effective and a limited greenhouse gas. The sun's energy is reflected from earth back into space as infrared radiation. Greenhouse gases interrupt this escaping heat and cause some of it to stay a little longer.

The infrared radiation leaving earth has wavelengths of between 0.6 and about 20 microns. Water vapour can intercept this radiation which has wavelengths under 8 and over 15 microns, and this accounts for more than 70% of the greenhouse effect. Wavelengths between 8 and 15 microns return into space without any significant interruption.

CO^2 operates very efficiently at the infrared radiation lengths of 4.102 and 15.589 microns, and with decreasing efficiency as the wavelengths vary out to 0.5 microns either side of this. If more than 0.5 microns either side of these key lengths, then CO^2 has absolutely no greenhouse effect whatsoever. See https://www.youtube.com/watch?v=57pU2F-bIQs for a full explanation.

What this means is that even if CO^2 were more than 400 parts per million, even if it were 4,000 parts, it could and never can intercept more than 10% of the heat escaping earth. This is all well known in geological science. Professor Robert Fagan's website shows the geological science at https://www.dr-robert-fagan.com/greenhouse-gases-the-co2-debate-and-sea-level-rise/ In the Cambrian period when CO^2 was over 2,000 parts per million, the earth's temperature was 3.5 degrees centigrade warmer than now. So why all the fuss and why is it believed?

One of the nice things about human beings is that in the main, they like to be "easy-to-get-along-with". They prefer to agree rather than disagree. When climate scientists either gang-up or are prevailed upon to pronounce that global warming threatens, two things are inevitable. One is that most will agree out of an instinct to conform, and the other is that the fear engendered will make the decarbonisers rich.

The Asch Experiment in conformity show that even when a correct answer is obvious to a subject, if six others all say something which is wrong, 37% of subjects will join them in answering with this obvious falsehood. When the untrue is less obvious, and is reiterated by a larger and seemingly unanimous majority, the truth becomes impossible for most subjects to see. A quick internet search for "The Asch Experiment" is a good place to start in understanding the utter credulity of persons when the majority proclaims a falsehood.

Another confirmation of the enormity of the power of conformity is provided by the Milgram Experiments conducted in 1961 at Yale University. A detailed outline and commentary on this experiment is at https://en.wikipedia.org/wiki/Milgram_experiment People conformed to authority even when it was causing intense pain to another person, or so they thought. It is worthy of being read in full.

Conformity is an enormous flywheel in social norms, and it makes us extraordinarily vulnerable to authoritative falsehood. Climate scientists (climatologists) have been seduced by the opportunity to put themselves at the centre of a threatened world, and pig out on the grants from a grateful population viewing them as saviours. They did not conspire in this of course, they simply acted in their own self-interest as they perceived it; just the same as the ladies in your common or garden-variety whorehouse.

We are not short of examples of science being complicit in falsehood, and sometimes it can be more implicit than complicit too.

Science tells us that gravity causes objects falling through a vacuum to accelerate at a rate of 32 feet (about 9.6 metres) per second per second. They fall through water at less than half this rate, and through concrete reinforced with steel much more slowly yet again. A concrete and steel structure which has borne the weight of its uppermost 20% for decades, may fall. It will however still exhibit some resistance. From one instant to another the Twin Towers fell down in free-fall time.

Fifteen thousand engineers and architects signed statements pointing out that this was not possible, other than when professional demolition is employed. And of course, it isn't. These people are heroes. Ninety-nine percent of scientists, however, were pleased not to notice this violation of Newtonian verities. Futile wars were fought on this unchallenged falsehood.

In Peter Ridd's book *Reef Heresy* he points out that Australian governments have committed $500 million to "saving" the reef. If 2% of these funds had been invested in auditing the "scientific" papers which stampeded this expenditure, it would have been shown to have been unnecessary.

Further, Australia spends $2 billion funding scientific research each year. If 5% of this, that is $100 million, was spent in auditing, verifying and replicating this research independently, then as much as 50% of it could be removed from policy considerations, and further, the charlatans and incompetents in science could be removed as beneficiaries.

That science is losing its standing in society is a tragedy, and unfortunately, this can only be addressed now by contributing to its humiliation. Only a humble science can be, indeed, great. Without the strictest adherence to truth in science, we are taken all the way back to alchemy, shamanism, and superstitious conjecture.

Let us get the oldest profession out of the newest!

PROTECTION: A JOB IN ITSELF

In the heyday of organised crime, "protection" was a racket perpetrated upon small business. Without the internet, businesses couldn't retreat into cyberspace to trade, had to maintain a shop-face, and were vulnerable to violent damage. An ugly, brutal, and intimidating practice against the vulnerable it certainly was.

Today, protection has taken a different form across myriad public functions. Increasingly, the objective of protecting one's job seems to take precedence over actually doing it. The degree and frequency of this modus operandi has crept into all sorts of work practices and seems to infest an alarming range of services. It manifests itself in all sorts of odd areas and seemingly without being noticed or commented upon.

The rationale is that if you don't make a mistake, you can't lose your job for it, and if you do nothing, you can't make a mistake. On the other hand, if your job description requires you to do something, if you do it to such an extent that it becomes a nonsense, you can't be said to be "not doing your job." The most obscure results abound.

For instance, farmers are now reduced to taking official weather reports with a grain of salt, if not outright cynicism. Why? Because if the forecast is for flood, tempest and hail, nobody in the Weather Bureau is negligent for not warning. Their jobs are safe. If farmers are promised flooding rains ten times more often than they eventuate, the forecasts are meaningless in practical terms and become guesstimates of great approximation. They are not the proper and best information, but manifestations of a job protection policy. One can no longer do sensible farming without deep cynicism.

In some areas "protecting you" takes on the most comic proportions. Financial advisors now must have complicated formal statements from their clients about risk aversion. These are mandated. On the face of it, and with many investors, this is of course, worthy of every consideration. Sophisticated investors, however, want brokers and advisers who will give them honest assessments. If they don't trust an advisor to give them the truth, they move on to discover one who will. They most definitely do not want their advisors vulnerable and inhibited by accusations of incaution. So, what do investors do?

On the mandatory forms they paint themselves as favouring the wildest possible speculative approach and options which the forms provide. They favour anything but this, but it enables the advisors to give them their understanding of the complete truth as to risk and reward. It places the advisor and client on a complete basis of trust, and releases the full truth as each understands it; this alone is the best approach in these types of decisions.

Sometimes protecting homebuyers from a "shoddy builder", has become a matter of protecting the shoddy builder. In one instance recounted by an honest though nonplussed builder friend of mine, no reinforcing steel at all was put into the foundations of homes built in series. The steel was placed into the slab and the building inspector signed off that it was there. It was then removed for use in the next building and there readied for inspection before the first building's concrete was poured, disguising the fact that it was not there. This was repeated thirty times. Since the builder could "prove" that it was there, it didn't need to be there. This was genuine protection indeed, but for whom? Nobody checked the slab with a metal detector because all were confident that they were "protected".

Science now affords widespread instances of "scientists" protecting their jobs rather than doing them. Incredibly, over 50% of scientific papers which have been "peer reviewed" are not replicable. Science which is not repeatable, and its result replicated, is not science at all. It is simply inaccurate if not fraudulent.

Professor John Ioannidis of Stanford University specialises in statistical research in health and medicine. His landmark paper "Why Most Published Research Findings Are False" has now been cited by thousands of concerned scientists. One quote may suffice:

There is increasing concern that in modern research, false findings may be the majority or even the vast majority of published research claims.... It can be proven that most claimed research findings are false.

The German drug company Bayer claimed in *Nature Reviews Drug Discovery* that 75% of the literature used for potential drug discovery targets is not reliable.

The prestigious magazine *The Economist* in 19/10/2013 commented:

A rule of thumb among biotechnology venture-capitalists is that half the published research cannot be replicated. Even that may be optimistic. Last year researchers at one biotech company, Amgen, found they could reproduce just six of 53 "landmark" studies in cancer research.

What is happening here? Researchers are protecting their jobs and their grants of public funds by doing "something". That something, though false, is sufficiently complicated and its thinking adequately in vogue to meet the approval of their peers who review it. Most modern research coming out of our universities, it seems, is no more than a protection scam.

It is highly possible however, that most of the people producing this rubbish are not aware that it is so. Fewer and fewer people are actually doing things like producing real products. It is only when one uses a tool that one discovers whether it is any good or not. The veracity of certain principles of bridge building cannot be known until a bridge incorporating those principles either falls down or fails to fall.

People who work in the abstract and never at the practical can have no concept that use alone defines value. If you have never actually done anything in terms of giving a practical outcome, all research and principles are of equal and indistinguishable value.

In a State or culture which believes that it must keep everybody busy (attain full employment) but can't suggest a specific object of the busyness (other than distributing wages income), the busyness itself becomes the object and assumes total significance. One rubbish result is as good as another.

The "protection disease" has now reached down to the menial levels of employment. Whether it is registering a second-hand trailer, building a shed, or buying a car, Government Departments, their staff, manufacturers, and clients are made to jump through a thousand hoops. Items must be stamped, supplied in triplicate, verified, authenticated, signed, inspected, witnessed, and often audited before productive activity is permitted. Trust and common sense are automatically assumed to be entirely absent.

The tedium of bureaucratic tyranny has been experienced by us all and is only welcomed by people with nothing else in their lives, and the strongest compulsion to see compliance as synonymous with virtue. You are not one of these, if you have noticed this tyranny of tedium.

Often, the only option is to exhaust the supervising authorities (and yourself) by complying with every triviality until no further means of providing protection can be conceived of. It can all reach outrageous proportions.

In many local governments now, there are eight people employed in administration for every one driving a grader, erecting a sign or filling a pothole. The application of this principle of protecting jobs rather than just doing them, may well hold the key to mankind's economic future.

Could the nirvana ever be reached where we are all protecting those attempting to do something until the ultimate bliss is attained whereby nobody can manage to do anything? Can the ultimate in safety only be had once total inertia has been accomplished and firmly secured? We can but try.

Yes, full employment is available despite technological advances and the automation of processes eliminating jobs. All that is necessary really, is that in the process of protecting our jobs, and complying with those protecting us, we all do as we're told. And do it willingly and determine to enjoy it too!

May we ask ourselves whether in the absence of trust anything will work, and whether there is then anything on earth which can make it work?

RIGHTS OF CENSORSHIP

The debate about censorship in the past centred upon the right of Government to censor and was mostly focused on the right to limit offensive language and pornography.

On the other hand, the right of those who own media to practice censorship has been sacrosanct. They can ignore whatever news they choose, and apart from libel laws, print what they like. As there is no law against lying (except a moral law of course), they can say almost anything and suffer neither censor nor censure.

The right to censor the news that Americans hear has largely been in the hands of the Ochs-Sulzberger family since they acquired the *New York Times* around 1900. A book published last year (2021) *The Grey Lady Winked,* by Ashley Rindsberg, walks us through how their right to censor American news has been used in the last 100 years.

In each of the "lines" that the paper chose to take, a particular reporter, or sometimes more, was chosen and promoted to contribute the stories and take the responsibility for them too, if the management sought to dodge it. What the *New York Times* told Americans has, on occasion, been most extraordinary.

That about ten million people were deliberately starved to death by Stalin's agricultural policies was never part of the NYT's news. Many other newspapers reported it, but not the NYT whose key Russian correspondent, Walter Duranty, denied it.

This newspaper was extremely soft on Hitler from about 1922 when he got out of jail, right up to the time when the "Polish attack" upon Germany started World War II. The NYT's correspondents Otto Tolischus and Guido Enderis were most prominent in Nazi apologetics.

A NYT's reporter, Herbert Matthews, discovered Fidel Castro while he was an unknown jungle-dwelling revolutionary without support, and publicised him until he won popularity and his Cuban takeover was accomplished. After he took over Cuba he came to America in 1959 and in 1995 attending a UN anniversary in New York, and both times attended the NYT and greeted and thanked the head of the Sulzberger family.

After President Kennedy negotiated a deal with the Diem government in Vietnam to remove 1,000 US military advisers in 1963 (which was done) and pull out all military advisers by 1965, it looked as though the coming war was not to happen. Then two NYT reporters stationed in Vietnam and with a near monopoly of reporting there, David Halberstam and Neil Sheehan, ran a protracted campaign imputing corruption on President Diem and several US Army personnel. This culminated in the assassination of Diem, and killed Kennedy's withdrawal deal.

NYT's science reporter William L. Lawrence, who in retrospect, was kept in the loop during the development of the nuclear bomb by the military, played the role of disinformation agent when the time came. The dropping of the atom bomb was reported in the NYT on 7th August, 1945. On the 10th of September he was reassuring readers under the headline "*No Radioactivity in Hiroshima Ruin*" and by the 12th September the NYT's headline read "*U.S. Bomb Site Belies Tokyo Tales*" and said the stories of radiation sickness amounted to nothing more than "Japanese propaganda".

With US soldiers returning from the Middle Eastern wars from 2002 on-wards, the NYT's reporter Jayson Blair wrote a whole series of articles on the psychological and emotional damage done to returned soldiers. The NYT's ed-itorial staff lapped all these up, even seemingly well-researched articles appearing

with a rapidity of one a day. Alas, these reports were almost wholly fraudulent.
Warnings from 12 months earlier were ignored and, in the end, it was a reporter
from another newspaper who blew the whistle.

Perhaps the *New York Times* overreached itself completely with "The 1619
Project". Named "1619" after the year when the first slavery ship came to North
America, it was begun by NYT reporter Nikole Hannah-Jones. Her opening
statement in the essay which launched it was "Our founding ideals of liberty
and equality were false when they were written." And also "Black Americans
fought to make [these ideals] true. Without this struggle, America would have
no democracy at all."

Rindsberg reports a whole series of bizarre NYT essays and persistent themes.
One asserts that American capitalism was formed by slavery, another traced the
failings of the present-day healthcare system to post-Civil War policies. Others
connected today's traffic jams to slavery in the South, and sugar-laden junk food
(yes even that) to slavery. In them even Abraham Lincoln was an unrepentant
racist, and as Hannah-Jones says, "Anti-black racism runs in the very DNA of
this country."

In trying to explain what allowed the wrongheadedness of the NYT to
"blossom" through the decades, Rindsberg suggests misreporting, distortions,
fabrication and "critical theory" type thinking. All these no doubt played a part,
but responsibility falls squarely upon the ownership.

From the beginning the Ochs-Sulzbergers have offered the public Class A
shares in their company. There is however a Class B of shares, and only these
have voting power, so the family, which has never sold any of these to out-
siders, has full control of the appointment of personnel and policy. While
the complexity of cause might be admitted, America's most influential news
media which plays something of a "policeman's role" over American expressed
opinion, is the preserve of the family which paid good money to acquire the
direction in which opinion in that country is guided.

The *Grey Lady*'s author finds it incomprehensively damning that a Jewish
family would repeatedly run material apologetic about the Nazi regime, which
he thoroughly documents, from 1922 to 1939. The NYT correspondent in

Nazi Germany was Guido Enderis, defended and excused by the Sulzerberger management through into 1941.

From one geopolitical perspective it is more understandable. By 1917 the Zionist movement had large support, and in the Balfour Declaration of that year, Britain had promised to give them Palestine, although at that time it had yet to be taken from the Turks. Establishing a national home for the Jews in Palestine was not going to be an easy matter. Zionism may have had much by way of media companies and supporting banking families, but an absolutely key ingredient to nation building had to be inserted into Palestine. People had to be persuaded to abandon a then-civilised Europe and take up residence in an Arab infested semi-desert or the Jewish State could never happen.

Before the protest at this becomes too shrill, another Jewish author, Edwin Black, and his book "The Transfer Agreement" published by Macmillan in 1984 might be heard. It reveals the agreement made by Zionism with the Nazis as soon as they came to power in Germany in 1933, to transfer Jews to Palestine. Under this arrangement 60,000 were induced to escape the antisemitism by emigrating to Palestine before the War interrupted the programme.

Could it be that European antisemitism was the indispensable harbinger of the future State of Israel? Of course, those Zionists who saw the value of Nazism in building Israel and gently abetted it, wanted it to threaten, but not more than that. The thing got out of hand, but few are critical of Jewish figures who wanted a little bit of Nazism, because they are barely acknowledged as existing.

It is easy to suspect that the strong anti-czarist sentiment in pre-revolutionary Russia was carried forward into supporting Walter Duranty's lying denial of Stalin's genocide in the NYT. Rindsberg evidences Duranty's private admission that the mass starvations did happen, and his dismissal with the words "They were only Russians".

Although it is difficult to discern, evidence and advocate some logical motive to other documented "strange" activities - such as encouraging Castro in a continuing relationship, undermining a South Vietnam Government, inventing false and contrived tales of disturbed US soldiers returning home, the United States Constitution being written and invented to defend slavery, alleging weapons of mass destruction, and denying that the atomic bombs dropped upon Japan had radioactive danger - there is a pattern here.   It is more than incompetence and misreporting; the mystery lies with the family ownership which "uncomprehendingly" allowed such to happen a little too often.

Rindsberg reports an incident where Arthur Sulzberger Jr was asked who, in a single combat between an American and North Vietnamese soldier, he would prefer to see killed.   He answered "I would want to see the American get shot. It's the other guy's country."

Still, the Sulzbergers paid good money to enjoy the right to largely determine what America thinks. So, who can deny them this? It's a free country, isn't it?

Perhaps the real problem is that, with enough prestige behind it, Americans will tend to believe anything, and telling them "anything" is just a family joke after all, rather than ideologically conducted warfare in the arena of public misinformation.

WHY DOES GOD SEEM SO SHY?

I once long ago asked myself the above question. If God is an all-powerful existent, and His wish is that we come to know and love Him, why doesn't He make Himself obvious? Many other existents seem to us completely obvious.

A case in point is the camel. He is neither particularly bright nor able, yet none would seem to doubt him. There is not to my knowledge a Camel-Atheistic Society bent upon denying his existence. Every person on earth, apparently, is convinced that the camel exists. Yet the camel shows no discernible interest in whether we believe in him or not, and indeed the millions of wild camels in Central Australia prefer that they not be noticed. Still, we believe. Even camel-agnostics are not in evidence.

In time I came to the view that God is perhaps both very thoughtful and wise. If God, all powerful as He is, were obvious, then our relationship with Him would be severely restricted. Most of us, being conscious that we are completely within His power, would immediately go into submission. For these of us, the only personal relationship possible would be one of the slave to the master.

Defiance would be an option of course, but only for the determinedly suicidal.

Obsequious ingratiation of the "yes Sir, no Sir, three bags full Sir" variety, would be every person's invariable and unalterable lot. It would seem therefore that God, if He be there as the all-powerful One which He must be, as this is in the very nature of God being God, may wish a different relationship from this one. What we schoolboys called "crawlers" for their embarrassing deference to authority are not, it seems, what are sought. The only alternative I have been able to conceive, is that God would prefer to have us as His friends.

At the end of Christ's stay with us, St John recounts His speaking of His disciples as His friends.

Would God create the universe, life, and humans, ultimately just to end up with some friends? Would He artfully never do anything in such a way as to make His authorship indisputable, always allowing doubt so as to enshrine the freedom of our will, lest we ascribe an arbitrary nature to God and rush to acclaim our slavery? From the "big bang" forward, for something like 14 billion years, he has always allowed us some doubt, and this in consideration of us, so that we would be able to volunteer Him our affections - for love can never be compelled.

This long and persistent insistence upon defending a measure of His anonymity as the author of all things would allow atheists to brand God as a reclusive fanatic, were it not for the restraining difficulty that they don't believe Him to be there at all.

He probably found it rather easy to 'leave us in the dark', as the expression goes, in the matter of the big bang; our utter inadequacies ensuring our stupefaction. Still, alternate speculations are to be had: a warp in time, the contrivance of a multi-universe making physics, and a riotous orgy of the strings of theory getting out of hand, among them.

We only very narrowly escape the tragedy of knowing with certainty of the existence of God when the likelihood of life occurring randomly is considered. Original life requires pre-existent proteins. These strings of amino acids average more than 150 long. With 20 different amino acids needed and available to choose from, their assemblage must then be uncompromisingly precise. The chances of getting the first 3 wrong are 20 x 20 x 20 to 1, or if you prefer it, random chance will get the first three wrong 7,999 times out of 8,000. Getting all 150 in the right order when there are 20 amino acids to choose from makes the chance of it being wrong 10 to the 70th power. As there are fewer than half that number of atoms in our galaxy, to give comparative chances, we would need to pick the only precisely correct one atom in two galaxies to mimic the chances of getting our one protein correctly assembled.

Though of course it is much more difficult than this. All amino acids come in right- and left-handed versions. Life only uses the left-handed ones, so even when the correct acids happen along, half of those too will also be wrong. Further, if the prevalence of amino acids allows another to be added in their making, on average, every X seconds, the desired protein will only last that long until another is added at one end, thus destroying it in its use to life.

Again, it is harder than this too. As the minimum number of different proteins is, as is thought, about thirty for the most primitive life to exist, then these thirty must randomly occur within touching distance at a particular transient moment. In the next moment, one may have added another amino acid, as they do, so the whole package is now faulted.

Even all this would be useless to life of course, unless information in the form of DNA were also present here, along with RNA which can read and act upon this information. A highly discriminating cell wall with powers to regulate entries and exits would also be necessary to encompass the whole.

Professor James Tour points out that interactors (special relationships within cells) are so excruciatingly numerous and complex that their probability of being assembled randomly and correctly approximates 10 to the 78 billionth power.

Another risky time came in the Cambrian period. While previously there were pretty much only single cell life forms, suddenly, in perhaps as little as ten million years, all animal body forms proliferated in the fossil records. This flummoxed poor Charles Darwin, who hoped that prior geological periods would eventually furnish evidence of these fossils' ancestry. This has never happened.

This sudden appearance of new life forms contradicts the gradual accrual of the small genetic changes of evolutionary theory. Just one might have been a surprising fluke perhaps, but suddenly there were dozens of completely new and different life forms. New DNA information as complicated as the Encyclopaedia Britannica just seemingly "popped" into existence for each of these novel life forms.

The so-called "Goldilocks" universe where all the forces, energies and elements are precisely calibrated to allow life, and differing them by a billionth part would end life on earth, is also seriously at risk of affirming intelligent design. The best rebuttal used here is that if there are a billion universes, then one will naturally be "just right".

That an intelligence would happen into existence by chance to be able to observe the phenomenal good luck of ourselves in being that intelligence, is another long-odds outsider that has come home.

The comforting thing about all this is that although the improbability of God's existence is again and again reduced to approximately infinity to one, in all instances the one persists. We can never be sure of God's non-existence, nor His existence either, and are thus prevented from abject submission, or to use the Arabic word for submission, 'islam'. Are we saved from this in order at least to allow us the prospect of becoming God's friends?

As love is always voluntarily given and cannot be otherwise, our lack of surety preserves our hope of friendship with God and allows us to love him also.

I don't doubt that surety is possible, but I do pray that it happens somewhere else under different conditions.

Whose were the words "My Lord and my God" but those of a doubter?

Fortunately, through all these near misses with certainty of God's existence, He has tenaciously preserved a small measure of doubt for us. We are not inevitably driven to be His cowering abject and destitute slaves with nothing to offer that He doesn't already have. Doubt preserves our right to offer the one thing that God doesn't already have, and never can have; our love - other than it being freely consenting and voluntarily given.

OK, so that's the meaning and purpose of the universe. What will we talk about tomorrow?

IF YOU REALLY HAVE HAD ENOUGH

If you are properly fed up with our politicians, what can you do about it?

Firstly, electing a decent one is an enormous job, and involves organising thousands of people. For now, that has to be put in the too hard basket. So what now?

There is a way in which 10 - 20% of voters can defeat all sitting members. Yes, this small number can easily defeat all sitting members of parliament. How?

Well, while it takes 51% to elect a politician, their winning margins are small. Many have margins of less than 5%, and few have more than 8%. If we put sitting members last, they can't get any preference votes, and they lose.

If most present politicians lose their seats, what will this do to future ones?

Firstly, they will notice. None will feel safe, and they will at last start to listen. This would bring the biggest "boil over" in political history, and whoever is elected will know it. It will be burned into their brains. They will know at last, that they must change.

But what if the new ones are no good either?

We will try something not very different. We put them all last too, in the next election. We must send politicians to school. If we pull their snouts out of the trough, expel them from the House, and throw them into the street where they will soon be forgotten, eventually budding politicians will get the message.

But why has it come to this?

Because the Politicians, Parties and Media have been training us in bad habits. We have been mesmerised mostly by two large Party groups. We are in the habit of asking ourselves: which of these is the worst? Then we vote for the 'least worst'. We always get the worst, but hopefully, we try to get the least worst. We're given a habit where 'only the worst will do.'

But what about exceptions?

If your politician has done his best to defend your freedoms and represent you, of course we make an exception. But any exception MUST be based on their record during their term in office, and NOT on their promises made at election time. If you haven't noticed their exemplary service, put them last.

Will this solve everything?

Of course not. It will take time for the politicians to learn. One brutal non-violent lesson may not always be enough. What we have to do is give them as many lessons as it takes, but something tells me it won't be many. The simple principle from which we need to start is

"Put Every Sitting Member Last".

Please share this good news with your friends right now.

PART FOUR

AGAINST TAKING THE RATIONALITY OF HUMAN BEINGS TOO SERIOUSLY

AN ORGANIC NINCOMPOOP?

O nce, a few decades ago, I was asked "What is man?" Of course, it was a different question then. Women were then automatically assumed to be part of the human race, and of mankind too. Now we are supposed to say "man and woman kind" or "personkind" to be inclusive.

Asking the same question of myself now, I will treat it as though it is inclusive of both sexes, as I have never doubted that it is. So, it is the same question. The answer though is different; today I am hypothesising that man is "an organic nincompoop".

The problem with thinking of ourselves as intelligent and rational, is that the conclusions we reach are also then thought of as being both intelligent and rational. We thought of ourselves as such when it was held that the sun circumnavigated the earth each day, and we still think of ourselves the same way when we contend the opposite; that the earth spins on its axis each day. Whether we are right or wrong, or just don't know; the one absolute surety we have had at all times, is that we are not nincompoops. A very comforting thought.

The United States has fought several wars and spent trillions of dollars fighting terrorism. We all take it deadly seriously. Since the 1960's when the US State Department began keeping the figures, the number of deaths from terrorism has been approximately the same number that have died from severe allergic reactions to peanut butter. The *Journal of Allergy and Clinical Immunology* puts US deaths from peanut allergies at between 75 and 124 annually.

It is estimated that before about 1700 when it fell out of fashion, between 40,000 and 100,000 women were put to death in Europe as witches. It must have worked as there don't appear to be any around now.

But that was then. We are smarter and more rational now, of course. The US and its allies have just killed more than 100,000 and spent twenty years and $10 trillion turning Iraq and Afghanistan into "democracies". How did that go, do you think?

Had it all been done because terrorists killed about 3,000 people in the Twin Towers and may well have had ideas of doing the likes of it again, it might have been painted as rational action. Alas, these poor souls lost their lives because in one moment of time, the bottom 80% of these reinforced concrete structures lost all resistance to gravity. They fell in free-fall time. The tops of these structures fell through their bottom 80% at the same rate as they would fall through air. The physics is absolutely clear. Only deliberate demolition is known to produce such a result.

Does this make us nincompoops? In the initial shock and disbelief some confusion may be winked at, but once the physics is observed and we choose to persist with the impossible, it clearly condemns us to nincompoopability.

Our stupidity is, however, both broadly based and wide ranging. Paranoia about "climate change" burgeons everywhere. CO_2 can only intercept 10% of the heat leaving earth; the infrared radiation within 0.5 microns of the wavelengths of 4.102 and 15.589 microns is all that is open to capture. Water vapour and CO_2 already capture about 80% of these specific radiation wavelengths. What CO_2 has already caught warms the earth by about 3 degrees Celsius. If CO_2 prevalence is doubled, and then doubled again, it may catch the remaining 20% and warm the earth a further 0.7 degrees Celsius. It would be difficult to notice except in the rising temperature of media hallucinations.[1]

---

1. See https://www.youtube.com/watch?v=57pU2F-bIQs for explanation.

Tesla, the electric car manufacturer, has recently issued a video explaining their progress at producing driverless vehicles. They make it clear that this demanded far more than was originally envisaged. As a result, once they have achieved their self-driving capacity, they believe that they will have discovered twenty times more about automating and robotising human functions than was their original intention. This will largely eliminate human labour from the economy. This is hardly evidence of nincompoopery, surely? Yes, but not so quickly.

The main spokesman for Tesla, observing that human employment will be increasingly swept away, suggested a solution; Universal Basic Income. This involves everyone getting a basic income irrespective of employment status or other considerations. It also involves a method of financing basic income. It is either to be funded by taxation or debt. That is, by removing take-home pay from those who still have some, or by adding it to what must be taken from take-home pay later.

The smartest people in the world cannot think of a way to increase people's income which does not involve taking income from them; either taking it immediately (today's taxation), or later, through debt repayments (tomorrow's taxation). If we give it to them and then take it back again, surely that will fix everything?

The smartest people in the world are very good at thinking about what they are paid to think about. What they are not paid to think about, it seems, they don't.

In technological areas they are given free range and every encouragement. In social areas of conceptual novelty, they are as confused as everyone else. One of the reasons for this is that large daunting road-signs are emblazoned across their paths. Like what?

A popular one says, "There is no such thing as a free feed!" This is axiomatic, universal and beyond contradiction. As it happens, we all break this "law" on a daily basis. How? An invoice for the DNA of an apple tree has yet to be presented. We were neither foremen nor workers on the capital works programme we now call the solar system. Whether the earth is an accident or the product of a careless creator who forgot to present us with the bill, we treat it as though we got it for nothing (and take care not to admit it).

Johnny Appleseed, apparently a simple-minded kindly fellow, walked the public roadways of America planting apple seeds as he went. He left behind, as his heritage to others, more than 50,000 apple trees by some accounts. Nobody paid Johnny a cent for an apple, they got them for nothing, but none could forgo the conceit, apparently, that they had all paid in full.

As our industrial inheritance advances, rendering our labour increasingly unnecessary - and even the presence of most of us at the site of production is superfluous, and most of the labour of producing the things which sustain us presently has been done by people who are now long dead - we cling tenaciously to the foolishness that "We did this!" Pardon me.

We live at a fault line. In geology, the conditions on one side of these is a complete break and at variance to the other. How so? Yesterday the unfaltering law was scarcity. Food, fibre, shelter, it was all scarce. Nowadays we are at more risk of the supermarket shelves subsiding to smother us, than at risk of not discovering their superabundance. Since the actual and real scarcity of goods is now unobservable, another scarcity is needed to comfort us in our age-old sureties. There is still a scarcity for sure: it is a scarcity of money to buy them.

Money is not a Godlike entity which resides with Zeus. It is most accurately described as a ticket system. A theatre ticket will entitle you to one seat at one performance. Dollars (or yen, euros, pounds etc.) entitle you to a certain value of an unspecified product-description. It is an artificially contrived claim, whatever its form, be it metallic, paper evidence of a claim, or a deposit recorded in cyberspace.

All such claims upon the economy have a legitimacy. If ever nations did accounts as do companies, they would record their assets and liabilities, as those things which afford a benefit (assets) and those which make a claim upon those assets (liabilities). All money therefore is created as a liability (a debt if you will) to the Nation's Balance Sheet, whether one has been drawn up or not.

When money is created it always, unavoidably, and automatically constitutes a claim upon our production and assets. If new money creations were distributed in equal measure to all, as a free gift, that money would still be a liability against the Nation's assets. Is it really necessary to insist that what is created as a liability to the Nation, must also be a liability to all those who receive the money? If we issued this money as a dividend or gift it would still also be a liability (to the Nation's economy), so it is not mistaken accounting.

Can we discover what society is doing economically, and have our symbolic system of money truly represent it?

An early tribe of ten persons decided to bake a cake. Some gathered seeds, others fruit. One milked a goat to moisten the mixture. Another stone ground the gathered grain. A clay pot was made by one to bake it while another gathered the firewood. In the end a cake materialised which may be described as a profit. These primitives then divided the cake and issued it to the tribe's members. Curiously, there was no debt. No tribal debt, no personal debt, and dumb Neanderthals that they were, no national debt either. Tomorrow morning began another debt-free day.

In those times, parrots were few and red parrots' feathers were hard to find, though they all thought that a handful of cake was well worth one parrot feather. In time they agreed that each of the contributions towards baking the cake; grinding the seeds, finding the fruit, making the fire etc., was worth so much in red parrot feathers. So now when the time came to eat the cake, it was doled out according to the parrot feathers earned in making it. Then one day the world changed forever. When all the handfuls of cake had been distributed for each red parrot feather, there was still some cake left over!

Mankind had reached the crossroads! The future for all times was in the balance. The tribe lost its cohesion and broke into factions eventually, but initially, being simple folk, they just divided the remaining cake and ate it. In those days people thought that the purpose of production was consumption.

Eventually of course it came to be understood that the purpose of the economy was to acquire parrot feathers, and to create human bother in the form of employment to a maximum extent. At first though, this was not understood.

The advanced thinking which brought this understanding took time to develop. It was a sense of justice which first led to this understanding. Why should everyone share equally in the profit of cake-making?

Tom had broken his leg and couldn't help so why should he get any? Dick just sat under a tree making strange unheard-of noises like "Rim, rim, spoke, hub, rim, spoke, axle, turn" and said he was "Doing inventing" but couldn't explain. While Henrietta looked after the children which has nothing to do with cake making. Surely their just portion is nil?

Of course, their crime of not contributing didn't warrant the death penalty, so what to do? You couldn't just give them the cake; they'd only eat it. Best give them the red parrot feathers, but give them as a debt to be paid back later. That solved everything. Every time a cake was baked at a profit, parrot feathers were added to the National Debt. Soon it could never be repaid, but at least we had justice.

In time the demand for parrots with red feathers was so great, and their hunting so out of hand, that all such parrots were extinct. The supreme intellect of man now came to "the fore as never before". If we can't have real feathers, perhaps *fiat feathers* will do it? Feathers became simply obligations to repay. Some were recorded with ink in ledgers, while others took up residence in cyberspace. The whole of the human economy didn't have a feather to fly with.

It was then that true justice was arrived at. The great mass of the lumpen proletariat could not see that the concept of phoney feathers had come to dominate the heights of human governance. Those of a higher intelligence had feathered their own nests. The cream, at last, had risen to the top. The justice decreed by nature itself had triumphed; all praises to it.

Viva la nincompoopery!

CONSPIRACY IS NOT TO BE ADMITTED UNDER ANY STINKING CIRCUSES

BY EDWARD MINTON*

I f men associate together for anti-social purposes, what are we permitted to call this state of association?

Clearly we cannot call it a "conspiracy" or we will be dismissed as "conspiracy theorists".

Either we must deny that any such associations ever exist or are possible, a proposition which no court would allow, or another word must be found.

Perhaps the word "*naughtiracy*" might suffice; in other words the association has a naughty intent; one which is anti-social. This does not imply that it intends to destroy all human wellbeing or impose a world hegemony, or is motivated by a conscious diabolical pursuit of evil of vast measure, of course, but it allows the possibility of saying that human association with a measure of anti-social intent is sometimes identifiable, though not of course with any allegation of *conspiracy* being associated with it. *Naughtiracy* is the much gentler word for those of delicate sensibilities.

Of course it must be allowed that there are differing degrees and definitions of both naughtiracy and the "C" word. Some believe that the "C" thing only exists when people associate together *in secret* for anti-social purposes. This places Nazism and Communism outside of any "C" connotation, as all was done in the open. Yes it is different in degree and scale, but not in principle to the players on a football field biffing each other in full view of all the spectators. It is a sort of biffing with a capital "B" perhaps, but is not con "C" ing surely.

Three or more hardened criminals associating secretly together to rob the local store have henceforth been designated as acting in "conspiracy". This is unfortunate and is the germ from which "conspiracy theory" burgeoned. Let us not speak of it thus; it is merely "covert-naughtiracy" and nothing more.

Defining "anti-social" can be a bit tricky also. For example, how are we to think of men secretly planning and executing the robbery of a bank? Apart from bankruptcies, theft from banks is pretty much the only time that credit is ever issued debt free into society. Those who advocate a national dividend for all when economies are profitable, may disagree with the methodology, but cannot see the result of successful bank robbery as being anti-social in all respects. I suppose it must be said that they are a-bit-of-a-naughtiracy.

You will have noticed that when we were told that about twenty Afghans organized themselves in a cave to steal planes and bring down the Twin Towers, this was not described as a conspiracy theory. If as many terrorists secretly detonated a stolen atomic bomb in New York and killed millions of people and started a world war, this too would not of course constitute a conspiracy; just another group of naughtiracists, though naughtier than most, it is true.

According to the post-modernist view, "good" and "evil" are simply terms of either vilification, or alternately an attempt to identify and exult a higher moral purpose. Such concepts as these can only emanate from value judgments, and these must be judged as highly suspect in the absence of absolutes which are now in the eyes of many, largely discredited.

In short, if conspiracy is associating together for evil purposes, it is a proven impossibility now that evil is agreed by a self-appointed coterie, not to exist.

*Poor Edward must be regarded as somewhat challenged by his age these days. Surely he meant "under any circum stanceses" and not "stinking circuses" at all.

CONTRACHONDRIA

So, what is it? We are more familiar with hypochondria which is a morbid condition characterised by depressed spirits, stress and anxiety about the state of one's health, and this irrespective, very often, of having very good health. Contrachondria, on the other hand, is a morbid and anxious condition characterised by depression and stress at encountering any suggested contradictions of one's group's consensus of opinion, and this irrespective of the truth or veracity, or even the blatant falsity of those views. Fear is an ever-present element of this condition.

It is very easy to diagnose as we all have it, though it differs in form and comes in various degrees of severity. Its onset is usually triggered when ideas at variance with views widely held are expressed. Whilst it cannot be cured in the sense of eradication from the human condition, its form can be altered and even overcome in some of its manifestations. An example of this happened in the 15th Century, and this lessening of contrachondria changed the world.

Off the coast of Morocco there is a reef, Cape Bojador, that runs one hundred miles out to sea. It is plunged in dramatic surf. European sailors of that time believed it to be the edge of the world, and none had ever sailed beyond it.

A younger brother of the King of Portugal, now known as Prince Henry the Navigator, decided to explore Africa. He funded thirty different expeditions to do this. All were afflicted with contrachondria and reinforced each other's fears of falling off the flat earth, so they found various reasons and excuses to fail. At last, in 1434 in an expedition commanded by Gil Eanes a barquentine-caravel became the first European ship to pass Cape Bojador by sailing well out to sea. The contrachondriacs were undone. In the following centuries Europeans navigated all the world and colonised much of it, changing the world forever.

A form of the fear of contrary notions afflicts the animal kingdom also. Sardines cling tightly together at the onset of predation, and herds and flocks move together in unison and tend to fear the safety of dispersal, even sometimes at their peril. Some such instinct may be at the base of human contrachondria.

Social people, though more rational, hold to the axiom that we are "better dead than out of fashion." It is not the particular fashion of the time, but the fact that it is the fashion, which invokes the fear of contrary dress.

With the help of our fear of change we have now developed a carbon-phobia, and most are alarmed at the prospect of climate change. Models of atmospheric carbon dioxide and the industry associated with promoting fear of carbon has been part of this; however, this essay is not concerned with how most became alarmed with the climate's future. We intend to show that there are several scientific observations which tend to discount much of this fear, but there is no interest in examining them. This is a pity and again, contrachondria would appear to be responsible.

One contradictory observation comes from geological research. Through geologists' knowledge of rocks, the level of CO^2 in the atmosphere during past ages such as the Cambrian Period is known to have been five times higher than the present 400 parts per million. The temperature was very little warmer when there was 2,000 ppm in the atmosphere. The most recent ice ages had higher CO^2 levels than now. Professor of Geology at the Kalgoorlie School of Mines, Dr Robert Fagan's website at https://www.dr-robert-fagan.com/ has all the data under Climate Change Unpicked.

Professor of Physics Dr Michel van Biezen of Loyola Marymount University, in his videos (one being https://youtu.be/57pU2F-bIQs of 9 minutes) explains the effectiveness and limitations of CO^2 as a greenhouse gas. While the heat (infrared radiation) escaping from earth back into space has wavelengths ranging from 0.6 to about 20 microns, CO^2 only operates within narrow wavelengths close to 4.1 and 15.5 microns. The total infrared radiation available to CO^2 interception is only 18% of the total. The major greenhouse gas, water vapour, already intercepts 70% of this, leaving only 5% as the total that CO^2 can intercept. Most of this, 3-4%, is already captured by the present level of CO^2, and even vastly increased levels can have little effect on atmospheric temperatures. This confirms the geological levels.

Resisting and ignoring this data can only be explained by contrachondria.

At times an idea may be so widely held that none can think to dispute it, even though it has no basis of truth. The belief that gold has high value is one such. No indispensable and unique use for gold has ever been discovered. Life is not possible in the absence of carbon, nor of the trace elements zinc, copper, selenium, chromium, cobalt, iodine, manganese or molybdenum. Gold plays no part in life.

Sometimes gold's property as a conductor which doesn't tarnish is acclaimed for it. There are a great many conductive elements and anyhow, electronics are not stored in corrosive environments. This property of gold is of no value unless you intend to throw your computer into the sea, or dip it into an acid bath.

That gold has high value causes us to want to display it. For the same reason however, almost all of it is locked away in highly secure vaults where nobody is permitted to see it. The mining of gold demands enormous inputs of energy and resources, its disturbance and damage to the environment is considerable, and in view of its absence of utility this is simply waste. Yet because of contrachondria, until this very moment of writing, it appears that none have suggested that its mining be outlawed. This would save us effort, energy and irreplaceable resources and protect us from folly, foolishness, and waste.

Warren Buffett, the famous investor, has calculated that all the gold ever mined in the history of the world, if assembled and put into a cube, would measure 20 meters high, wide and deep. It would fit on an ordinary house block. Because of the myth that it has value, until the early 20th Century attempts were made to ascribe all the world's wealth in terms of gold. This proved an impossibly inflexible currency and is now abandoned forever. If all the world's gold was removed to the far side of the moon, its impact on human life would be nil.

That we continue to ascribe value to it is wholly due to our slavish contrachondria.

One of the measures useful in addressing this malady is in confronting it. A challenging video which may be useful in this is on youtube at Evidence the Titanic Was Sunk on Purpose. It offers well-reasoned and sanely presented evidence that the Titanic did not hit an iceberg and sink in the North Atlantic. This invokes various reactions even though it does not claim to prove its hypothesis, and just gives the evidence.

The response "This is totally ridiculous, and I am not going to even look at such rubbish" is indicative of high levels of contrachondria. The reaction "OK I will watch it, but only to entertain my friends with the preposterousness of it" suggests a moderate level. "Let it float its boat and I will see if it holds water" is a mild one. Those exclaiming "I bet this is exactly right" have the highest levels of contrachondria and will be found to be associated with groups which have an abiding interest in conspiracy.

Another useful video is at https://www.youtube.com/watch?v=TIw1OPH 6QvM which tests our contrachondria. The historian, Dan Gibson, and many other academics too, now claim that the Prophet Mohammad was raised in Petra, and that in the whole of his life he never saw Mecca. This challenges all our accepted history, and the firmly held belief of a billion people. Amongst the evidence is that for a hundred years after the death of Mohammad, the direction of prayer in all Mosques (the kiblah) all pointed to Petra, not Mecca. Other evidence comes from the Koran. Again, a fear of contradictory data inhibits us from consulting it.

By 2021 the whole world was convinced that the only means of preventing deaths from Covid-19 was multiple vaccinations. We were so obsessive about this that effective treatments for it were not on the media's radar. Among the many testaments of treatments is https://rumble.com/vsokj8-dr.-shankara-ch etty-successfully-treated-4000-covid-19-patients-0-deaths.html from the South African medico Dr Chetty. His explanation is that the inflammatory phase of the viral infection beginning on day eight is, in fact, an allergic reaction due to viral debris, i.e., the spike protein. His recommendation of easily obtainable drugs such as promethazine (phenergan - you can get this antihistamine at any pharmacy in Australia without a prescription) to treat what is essentially pneumonitis would appear to be validated by his track record: seven thousand patients treated and ... not only no deaths, but no Intensive Care Unit admissions and no hospitalisations.

Good news is not news to contrachondriacs, it seems.

Perhaps the grandfather of all uncontested popular ideas, is that we are all sometimes able to make a little money. Not only do none of us make money through counterfeiting it, but no revenue from creating money increases appears in any Government budgets or accounts. All modern money is created in our banking systems, and usually by private banks. They create and own it all and only distribute it by renting it out to us at interest. Any money we have is always acquired from an original borrower somewhere. As a community, we owe every cent which exists.

The implications of this are that the elites which control money creation can readily acquire anything which money can buy, should they choose to do so. This enables the financial dependence of the major media to be arranged. The inertia of public misunderstanding of the private monopoly of money creation is greatly assisted to continue in this way, and given our affliction with contrachondria makes it nearly unassailable.

Any effort to democratise new money creations so that we, the country's true shareholders, can share in the benefits of it, would seem to await an increase in our knowledge of ourselves. If we can lessen our fears of believing what all others mistakenly believe, we may be empowered to pay ourselves a national dividend instead of continually increasing the national debt. A beneficial change in human wellbeing of the order of that which was forged by Prince Henry the Navigator nearly 600 years ago, may be offering. Accepting our vulnerability to contrachondria, and doing something about it, may be all it takes.

Perhaps it is only the truth which can set us free?

PREDETERMINING PERCEPTION

BY TOBY MALONEY, 1ST DEC. 2021

I think it now has to be conceded, in the light of the evidence, that thoughts are three dimensional. Thoughts may be somewhat flexible as to their shape, but they definitely exhibit volume. Measuring the size of irregular bodies is done with displacement. Thoughts have a displacement volume which, by occupying a place, preclude its "competition" or "opposition" from entry.

How could one possibly come to such extraordinary and unusual conclusions? It was done simply enough, by observation. Admittedly, the circumstances were novel.

During the 2021 pandemic in Australia, the government decreed all sorts of invasive measures. These upset about ten to twenty percent of the electorate quite considerably. Their grievances were varied. Some resented the restrictive lockdown, some the banning of the effective treatment ivermectin, some the compulsion to vaccinate in certain employment situations, some observed that countries with the highest vaccination rates such as Israel and the UK now had the highest infection rates, and Sweden with no vaccination, had the lowest.

We are not here interested in whether these people were right or wrong. This is irrelevant to our present purpose. The point is that at least 10 to 20% of people were cranky with government policy, and they went to rallies in the hundreds of thousands to express it.

Politically, with an election only four months away, the larger parties tried to ignore it. The small parties ran out in front of the mob, jumped onto whatever soapboxes could be found, and shouted "Vote for Me!"

If only 10 to 20% of electors voted for "me", "me" could not be elected. It takes 51% to prefer "me", to the 49% who prefer others, for "me" to win an election. The leaders of the minority parties thereby effectively disempowered their own supporters and ensured the revolt's dissipation. But what else could they have done?

10 to 20% of electors have it within their power to defeat all sitting Members of Parliament. How? It is so simple. You just put all sitting members last. Few sitting members have majorities above 5 to 10 %, so while it takes 51% to elect them, it only takes 10 to 20% to defeat them.[1]

The sitting members' replacements will then understand their vulnerability, and politics will be changed forever. If we can't elect a politician, as it were - and usually we can't - then why don't we defeat one to make the point? It's easier, and it certainly makes a greater impression on politicians' egos than just re-electing them. This is a *Politician Control Mechanism* (PCM). Most will agree that we need one.

All this would have come about in the 2022 election and put the electors back into control, except for a *predetermining perception*. What was it?

The thought was with the minor parties' alternate leadership. It was simply "You should vote for me", and as a thought it is quite voluminous. It has the ability to fill space and exclude other concepts and their possibilities. It may fit very snugly between the ears and bolster the brain up to the very brim. It is so self-serving and self-indulging, so comforting with self-importance, and so directs attention towards one's self, that it is usually not to be denied or neglected. Resisting this inner mantra of the mind, doubting its primacy in importance, or questioning this catechism of narcissism is predetermined in the negative.

---

1. Electorates which elect multiple candidates such as in the Australian Senate are different. House of Representatives Members are the vulnerable ones.

So the leaders of the minor parties again did the one thing they are especially good at: evidencing the dominance of the major ones.

THE ENORMITY OF CONFORMITY

YES, CONFORMITY IS A POWERFUL FORCE IN ECONOMICS TOO.

Those who conform invariably ascribe this to virtue; they never attribute it to a lack of courage or moral turpitude. It is always either one or the other.

The case for conforming begins with life. Children properly defer to the authority of their parents. Authority is properly and fruitfully deferred to however, only when it truly is authority. *Authority involves the exercise of power with responsibility, and is validated only in the context of love.* In a healthy family, loving parents have a valid authority, and one deserving of honour and deference.

The exercise of power in the absence of responsibility and outside of love as its context is unreservedly of the devil. If you don't believe in the existence of the devil or that evil can be real, this alters nothing of its actuality. To meet it is to know it.

Concurring in a lie knowingly is either cowardice or an act of hate. This too is conformity. Staying silent in the presence of lies or even untrue ideas sincerely held, is also dishonourable conformity.

In many areas of life without conformity there can only be anarchy. The classical example is cricket. The rules are the game. Without conformity to the rules, "it's just not cricket!" The competition is then one of winning advantage through cheating. But cheating at what? It is certainly not cricket.

If we cannot largely conform in conferring meaning in language, communication atrophies. We can then no longer follow the building manual for the Tower of Babel.

Weights and measures is another instance when conformity is of the very essence. Unless we agree on the mass of a kilogram, a kilogram cannot exist; just indeterminate mass.

Conformity can be a source of prestige, or its defiance a means of protest. Those who comply with the dictates of high fashion acquire a prestigious standing amongst their peers which is as transient as the fashion itself. Those who don't conform suffer from a lower social standing all the way down from raised eyebrows to ridicule, derision, and ostracism.

Efficiency in warfare is very much a matter of conformity in the lower ranks. In higher decision making its predictability brings tactical risk.

Slavery too was almost wholly a product of conformity, a fact which probably explains in large part why it took about seven thousand years from the beginning of civilisation before public opinion was resolved against it. This conformity was not just that of the slaves, but also the slave owners' concurrence with the social mores of their time, and that of free men who didn't own slaves as well.

The Asch Experiments in conformity show that even when a correct answer is obvious, if six others all say something which is wrong, 37% of people will join them in answering with this obvious falsehood. When the untrue is less obvious, and is reiterated by a larger and seemingly unanimous majority, the truth becomes impossible for a majority of people to see. The link https://www.yo utube.com/watch?v=NyDDyT1lDhA is a good place to start in understanding the utter credulity of persons when the majority proclaims a falsehood.

Another conformation of the enormity of the power of conformity is provided by the Milgram Experiments conducted in 1961 at Yale University. A detailed outline and commentary on this experiment is at https://en.wikipedia.org/wiki/Milgram_experiment People conformed to authority even when it was causing intense pain to another person, or so they thought. It is worthy of being read in full.

Conformity is an enormous flywheel in social norms. It is never broken or changed except through thought patterns differing, albeit that shifting circumstances may often have to prompt them.

As the believers in chaos theory would have it, it may take a butterfly fluttering his wings in the Amazon, to bring a man in London to change his mind.

In human affairs, conformity is the great Himalayan mass in front of reform and change. The enormity of conformity is such a factor in the human psyche that any change can be scarcely credible. Indeed conformity blocks all change and progress where numbers of persons are involved. This is why the future is always in the hands of minorities.

A minority of two persons explains why we are not all still riding horses.

Conformity is sometimes, when proof is physical, broken with minimal application. James Watt had an idea capable of demonstrating physically. With only the help of one other person, a medical instrument maker, he built a steam engine in his backyard. It worked. In the next twenty years he built twenty, and thereafter, especially as the external combustion engine became the internal combustion one, they proliferated everywhere. Many of us have three.

When it comes to desirable and useful change the majority is always wrong, because it is immovably caught in a pre-existent conformity. Change can only acquire consensus once it is a fait accompli.

Changing the world is all a matter of finding the butterfly in the Amazon which can do it. If it was 1776 and you wanted to reduce the number of horses in the world by 98%, what would you need to do? Go into your backyard and invent a steam engine, and that would do it.

Effective Reform

So what do we need to do if we want all new and additional money creations to be shared equally by all?

What we don't do is appeal to the majority to see that their nations are profitable, and that additional money regularly needs to be added into the economy, and that this ought properly to be owned by the citizens, and be distributed in equal measure to all. The majority will sleep through their disadvantage forever. The banks will retain their ownership of all money, only renting it to us at interest, with national indebtedness inexorably increasing every year. The bondage is ever to conformity.

Thales was an ancient Greek with a butterfly. He argued that all matter was made of water. His fellow Greeks vigorously contested this with a notion which became popular, that all was made of fire, water, earth and air. Some even contended that all was atoms. Today we speculate string theory and quantum theory. Thales began all this by contending the ridiculous.

If we wish to democratise the ownership of money creations, we will have to appeal to a minority to find and do a minimal thing, and thereby produce the necessary and desired consequences. Fortunately this "butterfly in the Amazon" has already been discovered.

All that is necessary is the application of corporate best practice to national economics. We need to produce the data which will lead, eventually, to the desired conclusions. This simple thing is the drawing up of National Profit and Loss accounts and comprehensive National Balance Sheets. These collations of data are widely understood because every company does them.

The National Profit and Loss Accounts would measure the supply of consumer goods and services, and set this against the effective demand from personal incomes. In this sense they measure supply and demand from the perspective of the nation's shareholders; its people. They may also be called National Supply and Demand Accounts for this reason. In normal periods a deficiency of demand (an inadequacy of personal incomes) will be evidenced. The reason for this may be left for now, but the fact of a recurring deficiency of personal incomes will be shown.

This deficiency accounts for the fact that the national indebtedness is continually rising. It has to, or recession results. This account enables central banking authorities to measure the amount of debt increase to avoid recession, and beyond which inflation will occur. Drawing up such an account is justifiable therefore, from a conventional orthodox economics standpoint.

Once a National Profit and Loss Accounts is regularly drawn up and has become a normal part of national accounting, the question as to why this deficiency of purchasing power has to be funded by creating additional new money as debt, will inexorably creep into consideration. Normally profits are distributed as dividends without debt to the shareholders. A National Dividend would liquidate production costs whether they were funded from debt or reserves, though it would reduce society's indebtedness instead of increasing it. This will become self-evident once the National P & L Account has a standing equal to the current Gross Domestic Production (GDP) calculations. Herein is the road to reform. Its truth will prove the way to freedom from ever escalating debt.

A comprehensive National Balance Sheet will reveal the net capital of a nation, and measure the growth or decrease in net national assets. It is a more useful measure than GDP, because this account only measures the total turnover and activity of the previous year; the actual outcome of which to national assets is not made plain at all.

Perhaps the greatest benefit to come from a Comprehensive National Balance Sheet will come from gaining an understanding of our national liabilities. A liability is anything which makes a claim upon our assets. The greatest claim upon national assets is the national money supply.

As things are now most politicians believe that if they sell national assets for an increase in the money in the country, they have done well. They have simply decreased our assets and increased our liabilities. It is true that when a national asset is sold we gain foreign exchange, which is an asset; however counterpart funds have to be created to pay the seller, so the net result is one asset less, one asset more, and one liability more. The worth of our balance sheet is reduced by the amount of the sale.

While exchanging surpluses with other nations makes good sense, a "favourable balance of trade" depletes our national balance sheet by a like amount.

If we are ever to empower our people with the proceeds of our national profit (the consumer goods produced above the recompense paid as personal income to induce that production) we shall have to measure that national profit. Something, indeed anything measured, is something proven to exist.

Once we have measured and acknowledged national profitability, and only then, will our options in using, sharing and distributing it become apparent. Under the inertia of conformity we have disenfranchised ourselves from access to national profit, only to see it grow in cyberspace as accumulating indebtedness to our banking system.

The natural beneficiaries of national profit are its people, and with the leverage of our industrial inheritance and technology, it is increasingly large. A prototype National Profit and Loss Account has been done, and showed that in the United States in 2014 it amounted to $7,500 per person, or $30,000 for every family. This account is available, though it is highly technical, at http://www.socialcredit.com.au/uploads/NationalAccountsPrototype.pdf

A similar profitability is demonstrable in all other advanced countries too.

An enormity of conformity is denying people everywhere their natural right to direct the economy to serve them in a manner of their own choosing.

Who could have imagined that a set of accounts could empower people in their own economy to something like $30,000 per family per year? Almost nobody, surely, until the butterfly flutters its wings.

THE PRE-EMINENT PANDEMIC

No personality in history has had such attention in literature and on screens as has Covid-19. It is not just the volumes of scribbles and comments, but the variety of the virus's attributes both alleged and denied which overwhelms. I can find nothing within my imagination which has not been said of it repeatedly, and disputed, and this in every conceivable variation. Fortunately, my interest does not lie with the virus, but with the other organism.

If one drops a bomb amongst a flock of guinea fowl, the guinea fowls' attention will be wholly focused upon the bomb. Those absorbed in observing the mysteries of organic beings' behaviour will find it is the guinea fowl which offer the greater interest.

The contagion of fear was the first phenomenon. Although it never happened, there were well received and believed stories of uncollected bodies lying in the streets of Wuhan. The rush to treat the infected suggested ventilators as a treatment followed, which, as it happened, exacerbated the tendency towards blood clotting and increased casualties appreciably. Next came "A vaccine, a vaccine. My Kingdom for a vaccine!".

Traditional vaccines have been phenomenally effective against bacteria like smallpox. Poliomyelitis had been banished into only Afghanistan and Pakistan by 2018 and 2019, where vaccine-derived polio was twice as prevalent as the wild virus. It is conceivable that even there, it may be banished at some point and suffer extinction as did smallpox.

Fortunately, the polio vaccine could be used where the infection was not present. This not only prevented its entry, but it also separated the virus from the recently infected or vaccinated, and any only partially immune people. The opportunity for the polio virus to mutate into more infectious or more vaccine-resistant strains, was not therefore offered.

The panic to vaccinate for Covid-19 is of a different order. Professor Geert Vanden Bossche is a vaccinologist and led the international team which produced the vaccine for Ebola. In my words, what he is saying goes something like:

"Giving antibiotics is always kept as limited as possible to reduce the possibility of the bacteria developing immunity to the antibiotic. Giving covid vaccines to hundreds of millions of people in the midst of the pandemic is guaranteed to offer the ideal conditions for mutations into more virulent and more infections variants to occur. Thus there are active viruses in many thousands of human bodies at the time of vaccination, and mutation can occur in as little as ten hours."

The variants are certainly coming fast enough. The most inoculated populations on earth with over 99% jabbed, Israel and Gibraltar, now have the highest infection rates in the world. Why? Because new variants are repeatedly occurring there and the whole population is without immunity to them. Deaths and enduring ill health from the vaccinations themselves, is also increasingly acknowledged.

While this is well enough known, the guinea fowl are too busy cackling in the trees. Their one object is to feel good. Most feel best when they are virtuously compliant, and have a reassurance of safety delivered from that surrogate parent for adults, the mass media.

The attainment of conditions most conducive to producing new variants is a win-win situation. Pharmaceutical companies make extra sales, and governments get more accolades for protecting us. Those who can convince themselves of the efficacy of masks and "distancing" and lockdowns, or who don't question them, have the warm inner glow of the compliant good. As Professor Bossche has observed, with constant mass vaccinations for the ever more variants this produces, the pandemic can become permanent. Once pandemics used to pass in time. Now their duration is only governed by the virus's ability to mutate in the most favourable and widespread circumstances which we provide them.

Perhaps the most frightening thing about the pandemic, is that we guinea fowls prefer emotionally inspired thinking about it. Compliance is ever deemed as virtuous, while critical thought is disturbing, fails to reassure, and predisposes us to stress; so, it must therefore be wrong.

Bossche says vaccinate the most vulnerable, by all means. Concentrate on giving the best care available to any infected, but vaccinating the lowest risk persons (which is certainly most of us) is a recipe for disaster. When both Governments and the media get it wrong, bitter experience is the next reality check.

The new variants will cease when we stop assisting them into existence. Since we seem to be unlikely to stop it, I am also unlikely to be proved wrong.

India has markedly reduced fatalities through the widespread use of ivermectin in treating infection. The Western media views this information as being counter-productive to the campaign to increase vaccinations and chooses to suppress it.

Scepticism, rather than comfortable compliance, would seem to be in order.

THE PEDIGREE OF MONEY

A CYNICAL EXAMINATION

There is a beginning to all things. Even money is not eternal. It begins somewhere.

Where money comes from is easily explained. *It is conceived in iniquity and borne in debt.*

How so? Well money can and does command all that money will buy. In the beginning nobody works for it, or gives up anything else to get it either. It is just created. Created? You mean just like God? Exactly like God! This is why atheists believe that all money grows on trees; they don't believe in creation.

It is conceived in iniquity because all money results from theft. If you grow a cabbage or weave a basket you own these things. If you create money, you can claim these things without any real thing having been offered in exchange. Your product is your claim upon products, though it is no product at all. Please relax. It can only get worse.

If you want me to explain I will simply not do it. If you have come this far in life and have never wondered who creates all of our money, owns it, rents it out to us at interest, and buys all that money can buy (which of course includes 90% of all media) we can't help you, I am sorry. You will need to plug your brain in at the wall first.

Most bankers are pathetic little bean counters and understand zilch about what the hell they are doing. When they give a loan, nobody's deposit is lessened, but the deposits of the payees of the loans are increased. Moral outrage at this practice has long passed its use-by-date, as it all started in 1694 with the establishment of the Bank of England.

Of course it all revolves around how one conceives of iniquity, or of iniquitous conception. If acquiring the product of another by costlessly creating a claim upon that product is not, to you, fraudulent, then relax, join a bank and live with luxuriance.

So much for the *Conceived in Iniquity* part of the formula. But what of the *Borne in Debt* part?

Money is always borne without gender, but it is not necessarily borne without polarity. A number may be positive or negative, be a credit or a debit, a plus or a minus number. Money is now purely digital, its existence being wholly in cyberspace as an enumerated abstraction.

In the beginning the banks, which create all modern money, created it and loaned it out wholly to finance production. It was all distributed as a debt owing to the Banks by the producers who borrowed it.

This was a necessary discipline in the economy. If the public was prepared to buy the product for more than the bank loaned to the producer, the debt could then be repaid, and the next cycle of production could begin. Those producers who could not produce more value than they consumed in doing so, would ultimately go out of business. This insistence upon either efficiency or bankruptcy brought capitalism to global triumph and its establishment as the dominant economic system was assured.

When capitalism reached perfection, and every producer produced more value than he consumed in the course of production, so that prices were more than incomes, not just production had to be financed with increased debt, but enough consumption also to keep the system going. Economic convulsions appeared, recessions, economic downturns and ultimately severe depressions erupted, so there was no option but to crank up debt to also fund consumption.

Once consumption had to also be financed by increased debt there was no road back; we could only go forward with increased debt every year or recession would result. This was the Keynesian "solution".

This efficiency of capitalism was actually measured for the year 2014 for the US and this showed how far capitalism has come. Consumer production was $2.4 trillion more than consumers' incomes and this amounted to a profit of $7,500 per American, and $30,000 per family of four.

http://www.socialcredit.com.au/uploads/NationalAccountsPrototype.pdf is the link which displays this. By 2014 the US economy was so efficient that its consumers' incomes were insufficient to buy their own production by $7,500 each that year. So did all this production stay on the shelves and rot? No; because it was managed in the usual way. Well how?

The total indebtedness of Americans was increased that year by $2.3 trillion. Actually the debt didn't have to increase at all, provided that consumers' purchasing power did. This could have been done by distributing some debt free credit, or a national dividend for that matter. This, however, would have violated the financial system's maxim that all money must belong to it, and only be rented out to society.

In this way the profitability of our economies compels total indebtedness to increase each year. The USA's debt now runs at over $90 trillion, and the world's at over $200 trillion. When people are organised under capitalism they are efficient; they produce more than they are paid to do it, and they can't therefore buy the extra goods without increasing their debt to the banking system to bring more money into existence.

The world is going bankrupt to finance its own profitability. I suppose it is easier than creating some money which is not debt. I suppose also, that there may be intelligent life in outer space, but how much do we have here?

Oh stop it! My head hurts! And I am not going down that road! Debt without any other option is what we have; opposing it demands thought and effort. Establishing political democracy took hundreds of years. Economic democracy with some economic votes being distributed freely because our country is profitable, will take us just as long. So best go and tell someone else, old mate, your words are wasted upon me.

Yes I will do that. Thanks for the encouragement.

PEOPLE, AND THE FLOCK AND SHOAL FACTOR.

D ecades ago I spent some months in the "budgerigar country" of far Northern Australia. These birds would assemble in huge flocks; perhaps even at times exceeding 100,000 strong to come to the water holes. Not that they could ever be counted. One photographed the flock and then estimated density.

The most amazing and mystifying thing with these flocks is that they acted as one. Continually whirling, veering left or right, swirling down or up or about in unison. There was never any evidence that one moved and then others followed. Multiple thousands moved instantaneously, as one, and in perfect coordination, and without any apparent communication one with another.

Mostly these sudden and well-coordinated manoeuvres were without any apparent cause or purpose. At times a move may be dictated from without the flock, by such as a hawk attack, though without a hawk in sight the flock would stagger and convulse about through the air far more than the drunkest of sailors.

A shoal of fish is similarly organized; a fact which is exploited by the many sea predators, and shows the sardines' surety that safety is in numbers. A concept of safety which often allows dolphins, tuna, sharks and the like to hold the school together until the very last one is eaten.

The complete coordination of their instantaneous movements in unison is just as impressive as that of the budgerigar flocks. Attempts to explain this are sometimes made on the basis that fish live in a conductive medium, which of course is water. Water dwellers from sharks to pelicans and platypus, are known to detect the presence of prey by electrical detection of the voltage of the preys' bodies. So perhaps the extraordinary coordination of fish shoals is done by communicating via electrical signals?

Of course the budgerigars don't have this option as they live in air, which is an electrical insulator rather than a conductor. When there is no external threat, we simply don't know how they coordinate themselves. Coordinated consensual effort, action and thought, where the external environment does not suggest it, are a thus far unfathomable phenomenon. But is it confined to birds and fish? Lemmings and wildebeests have migrations and mass movements which may suggest it.

Robert Ardrey inquired into the territorial acquisitions of animals, and found that they are universal throughout nature. Mammals, birds and even worms insist upon having a territory in their social organisation. This predisposition towards real estate is common to all creatures, as his work "The Territorial Imperative" shows, and man is not an exception.

Is the spontaneous swirling of public opinion towards common ideas, or against them, and the surge and subsidence of popular human movements an echo of the unanimity often shown in the lower life forms in their universal, though inexplicable choices of directions? Although we risk giving offence to the human race in imputing irrationalities to it, the idea is worth a look.

CO_2 is now a public enemy, and every climate model done in the last ten years, has predicted that the climate would now be warmer than it is. We are all acting in unison, and with unanimity, whether scientists or laity, on the basis that CO_2 offers a threatening global warming. The science for global warming is said to be incontestable. But what is the science?

CO_2 is both an efficient and limited greenhouse gas. It operates by grabbing the photons of infrared radiation attempting to escape back into space, vibrating, and emitting the heat in random directions into the atmosphere. This of course retains atmospheric heat quite efficiently.

CO^2 however, only intercepts very limited wavelengths of infrared radiation which has a range from .065 to about 20 microns. The wavelengths intercepted are 4.102 and 15.589 microns. Water vapour acts as a greenhouse gas at all wavelengths of infrared radiation below 8 and above 15 microns, so is competing with CO^2 at its wavelengths.

CO^2 will also grab infrared wavelengths in close proximity to 4.1 and 15.6 microns, though never more than 0.5 of a micron away from them. Between water vapour and CO^2 at 400 parts per million, the radiation between 3.6 and 4.6 microns, and between 15.1 and 16.1 is nearly all now captured. The logarithmic factor with CO^2 which is not disputed scientifically means that if CO^2 doubles (from 400 to 800 ppm), then the temperature (other things being equal) will only increase about 0.3 degrees Celsius, and were it to double yet again to 1,600 ppm, the increase would be no more than another 0.3 degrees.

The geological records confirm this. The Professor of Geology at the Kalgoorlie School of Mines, Dr Robert Fagan's work confirms this. Most ice ages have had higher CO^2 levels than exist now, and the Cambrian period which saw the greatest explosion of life ever, had CO^2 levels above 2,000 ppm and a temperature barely warmer. The full facts are at Dr Fagan's website: https://www.dr-robert-fagan.com/greenhouse-gases-the-co2-debate-and-sea-level-rise/

While this is known and accepted, it is irrelevant. The flock and shoal factor has decreed that we will wheel away from CO^2. One is usually met with resentment for mentioning or explaining this. The inexplicable urge to do as the others do, is upon us, and anciently acquired conformity is still present and masterful. The scientist is no more immune to this than the dullard.

Examples worth considering abound. Like everyone else I was appalled at the treatment of George Floyd by the police. George called out thirty times "I can't breathe....I can't breathe ...I can't breathe....etc." Months later I tried yelling this out myself. I couldn't do it twice without another big lungful of air. George convinced us that he wasn't breathing. Somehow he got onto that wavelength that convinces in a "flock/shoal reacting" sort of way. No one who is out of breath can yell something thirty times.

Most of us have observed objects falling. We've dropped something off a house roof or down a stairwell. We know that bricks fall at an acceleration rate of 32 feet per second per second. Yes, through air they do, but not through water. Water offers some resistance. The only objects which descend at "free fall" speed are those not encountering any resistance.

So how is it possible that the Twin Towers fell at free fall speed? The upper stories met no resistance as they fell through the concrete and steel of the lower ones. Ten thousand engineers and architects have signed statements that this is impossible without deliberate and well executed demolition practices. Just another irrelevancy! The facts are not a consideration when the budgerigars have somehow determined to move. Our instinctual reflexes are engaged and none can be left out of the moving mass mind. Fear and resentment are the lot of those offering logic. The stampeding herd is always sure it is "right".

I suspect that there are people somewhere selling this type of knowledge to advertisers. If the budgerigars can be induced to "take off" the mob will spend millions, and perhaps not even know why. Surely fashion companies like Nike know all about it. Budgerigar boots?

It seems highly probable that those working at the highest levels of politics are cognisant of this. Five lobbyists are employed by financial interests for every US Congressional Representative. In spending this sort of money to lobby and influence, it is most likely that they are doing it well, and exploiting every psychological advantage.

Could it be that the above examples of people acting unanimously, instinctively, instantaneously, in unison and with conviction at variance with logic, facts and known science, are but the tip of the iceberg? Does the human mass-mind follow the flight paths of the budgerigar? An understanding of the acting organism eludes the birds themselves?

Is it like this for all organisms? Even for man himself? Can anybody explain fashion fetishes; why the French went into revolution, the Russians into communism and the Germans into Nazism? It did none of them any good, and we see it in retrospect as nonsensical. Oh yes, we invent reasons. Far be it for men to acknowledge compulsive irrationality as a feature in common, at least periodically in the collective, with all other organisms.

The budgerigars' exhibition of this is the most beautiful and wondrous. In the light of early morning, beside the lonely water holes, in the green and gold of their millions, they repeatedly display perfectly co-ordinated dancing without any rehearsal.

Is it permissible to consider human beings in the collective, as strange organic phenomena, ever given to transitions in the norms and fashions of collectively shared thought patterns, and this largely in disregard of logicality? Are we governed by some deep ancient herd orientated instinct; beyond conscious thought and not only undiscoverable, but even unsuspected in the subconscious? A submariner governor in the collective mind which has driven the imperative of a folk impulse towards conformity time out of mind, and un*mind*ful of the suasion of the conscious, the rational or logic?

What defences does our organism have; how can this thing be bound back from excess and a descent into true madness? If such exists, it might lend credence to the above thesis.

The Latin word *ligare* is the root word of ligament; that which binds. It is the origin of the modern word *religion* too. Cicero's sense of it was "scrupulous or strict observance of the *traditional cultus*".

That religion has been part of every human society is a fact that even atheists would not deny. This indicates an awareness in some way that a "binding back" is needful. An ideology may serve here as the binding, but this only reaffirms the universal acknowledgment of the need.

The tragedies of the Twentieth Century are but the most recent affirmation that men are never far from the vulnerability to collective madness. The only defence is in putting aside a false pride in our political correctness (which is a different thing in every generation), and acknowledging the persistent existence of *the budgerigar factor*.

Implications of the Budgerigar Factor

Some will dispute the idea that inexplicable behaviour is a fixture in organic creatures. They hold that for a long time the homing ability of pigeons was a mystery, for instance, but it is now established that there is an ability in pigeons to detect the earth's magnetic field. This has been shown by attaching magnets to pigeons' heads and this does disorientate their direction finding. But the mystery does not end there.

Early mariners had compasses which always showed north and south. By shooting the angle to the sun at noon (its highest elevation) they could tell how far they were from the orbit of the sun.

But this didn't really help at all in calculating latitude if they didn't know what day of the year it was. For example if the Sun was directly overhead, they would be at the tropic of Cancer if it was the 21st of June, and at the tropic of Capricorn if it were the 21st of December. If the Sun was directly overhead at noon on any other days, they were somewhere in between. If the pigeons didn't have a reasonably accurate 365 day calendar they could know practically nothing about latitude. The Sun's orbit around the earth moves 5,166 km north and south according to the season. The pigeons' spatial sense is thought to be of greater accuracy than an approximation within 5,166 km. So the pigeons need to have both a compass and a calendar to have the ability that they demonstrate.

These told the mariners their latitude, but it didn't tell them where they were, so the course to a desired destination was not established. It gave latitude but not longitude.

Longitude was first solved by using an accurate chronometer set to Greenwich Mean Time. By comparing this clock's time at the time of their noon it gave their position east or west of Greenwich, so longitude was established.

So how do pigeons and migrating birds know their positions in an easterly and westerly direction? Alaskan plovers fly to Hawaii for winter. It is 2,500 kilometers nonstop, and if they are out by even one degree they never sight Hawaii and die at sea. It is not a due south course. Their means of knowing longitude is still a complete mystery. They have to fly to a fixed variant to due north and have only instinct to determine what this variant is. They don't begin from a fixed location, so the angle of variation has to be adjusted accordingly.

Pigeons can be taken in darkened cages which rotate one way, and then another, to all points of the compass, yet they still have a sense of longitude. If pigeons are taken to points either due east or west of their homes, can they measure the time spent in these darkened rotating cages designed to disorientate, and upon release determine the time of day at their release by the position of the sun relative to due north, compare it to their time of departure from home, and determine longitude? Probably not, and they have to know where they are and where they came from both latitudinally and longitudinally to always know the direction to home.

Pigeons need a compass, a calendar and an accurate clock to know as much as do men.

There are deep mysteries in the behaviour of organic creatures. The ability of budgerigars to move instantaneously, unanimously, and in perfect unison and without any detectable or observable means of communication or external prompting is one such mystery.

Do men, as a collective, have such behavioural inclinations? It would seem so; both in matters of fashion in dress and in politics, and also in acceptable societal norms. Is there an unobservable though strong instinctual vulnerability to suggestion buried somewhere in us and influencing human behaviour? If we answer this with a "yes", its implications take us to a strange and unfamiliar place.

The nature of instinct is itself shrouded in mystery. That a house-trained dog will instinctively chase a rabbit on first sighting one, is acceptable as instinctual. To explain that there is much more to this compels me to tell a true story.

Angus McDowall spent his semi-retirement on a small farm out of Toowoomba. He bred kelpies and sold them to Dutchmen. How come? Tulip farmers know that ducks will not eat tulips. To clear the tulip fields of weeds and insects they truck in thousands of ducks for the day. That's easy, but how does one get the ducks back onto the trucks that evening? Sheep dogs do it with ease.

He put an antique tractor on the market and it was bought by a fellow from Sydney, who came up to get it and camped for a couple of days. In the morning he was walking his three yellow dogs on leads and Angus told him this was not necessary, and was assured that it was. No it's not. Oh yes it is. And that is how the story came out.

These were purebred dingoes, bred in suburban Sydney for five generations. None had ever killed their own food, nor had any even seen a kangaroo in these several generations. He was walking them without leads one day along the edge of one of Sydney's large area parks. Suddenly there was a kangaroo nearby in a large treeless area which backed onto a bushy park. His dogs immediately gave chase.

He yelled "Come here, come back!" to no effect. After a while he realised that his yelling would attract attention from the neighbouring houses, and then he would be in devilish trouble. He had to shut up, so he quietly sat down and watched the proceedings in silence.

The first thing he noticed was that one of the dogs had disappeared. The other two put themselves between the roo and the bushy park into which he sought to escape, and wheeled him back and forth as the roo sought to circumvent them. In fifteen minutes or so the two dogs and the roo were exhausted and standing still. The dogs in front of the roo and on either side, and the roo facing them and all of them panting laboriously.

At this point the third dog reappeared from the grass five meters behind the roo. It ran up the roo's back, seized him by the neck and broke it.

That dogs will chase roos from instinct is not the point here. From whence came the plan and perfect execution of the two dogs exhausting and delivering the roo with precision into the third dog's killing field most advantageously?

Without practice, experience or habit these mature dingoes knew their stuff, and this after being isolated from any means of learning it for five generations. The *emotional* thing "Let's chase kangaroos" is very understandable. The *intellectual* thing of its military execution to perfection without practice or training, takes us to another level altogether. It appears not only to be an innate emotional instinct, but an intellectual legacy for its planned achievement as well.

Where could the intellectual content of their ability come from if it is not stored as an emotional drive?

No poodle, Labrador or Alsatian has this. If dog breeds are not the same instinctively, are peoples sometimes different too?

Is it possible to contemplate a humanity which will someday accept that their social norms often arise from unknown and unknowable collective herd sources? This grinds against our every impulse to be in control; I know what is going on; and then grabbing something from the air "And this is the cause of it", we take ourselves back to surety. If this is how we handle it, then we are only affirming our ignorance. And worse still, we are avoiding and neglecting a search for and consideration of the truth where it lays.

In the human organism, explaining the flights of whole peoples into one "ism" or another periodically, taxes out resources of explanation. The media is a popular culprit, though it quickly evolves into the centralisation of the control of major media. From here this brings us to the role of money and bankers in centralising it, and thereafter comes conspiracy.

Everybody, of course, believes in conspiracy. If three men appear simultaneously at a bank and proceed to rob it, this is not usually put down to coincidence. As conspiracy is defined as "cooperating together for evil (antisocial) purposes", then the only grounds upon which conspiracy doesn't exist in this instance, is that robbing banks is morally OK, or that the three robbers acted independently and without knowledge of the other.

Once we have division as to the nature of good and evil, we also divide on the objects of association on this basis. As each sees the intent and purpose of the other as not being OK, they attribute conspiracy to the opposing party. If everyone else is a conspiracy theorist, though they themselves are not, it is now a "definition of conspiracy" debate.

Is there a big question we should be asking ourselves here? Beyond the media and advocacy, politics and law, money and the private monopoly of banking's money creation, is there another undiscussed and ignored control; the biological?

Why does each generation believe patent falsehoods? The propensity to give credence to falsities varies only it seems, with the specifics of which ones.

Malcolm Muggeridge put forward a logical motive for illogicality in collective mores and attitudes. Speaking in April 1979 at a Center for Constructive Alternatives function in Michigan, and as reproduced in the May, 1979 issue of *Imprimas,* the motive was definitely not survival, but rather its opposite. The topic he had given his address was "The Great Liberal Death Wish" a topic he said "I've given a lot of thought to and have written about..." He cites fifty million abortions as the global annual figure, increasing legislation for euthanasia, and soaring drug taking in his evidence for society's craving for suicide.

It would seem that the mystery motive for much of our "correct" attitudes is, arguably, self-hate and denigration in some sort of death wish; at least in Malcolm Muggeridge's estimation.

We know that endless repetition is very effective in advertising, but influence over the public mind is not a matter of rapidly talking over the top of each other to win the argument.

Shock, surprise and fear are effective in shifting opinion as the fall of the twin towers showed. Only one person in my acquaintance, an engineer, saw it for what it was immediately. He knew that a quantity of concrete and steel with a mass of X, cannot fall through a mass of concrete and steel equal to 3X at free fall speed. I was much slower at seeing that this was so.

One can convince people of something if you can convince them that others are convinced. The herd instinct to conform is always there, but why is it so strong? The idea that unity is strength is a two edged sword. If by uniting you are weaker than the enemy, you have for his convenience presented all that you have to him in one place for his ready dispatch. If you are weaker once united, your best strategy is guerrilla warfare, dispersal, safe refuge, and the seeking of local advantage.

Until the 1st Century AD, no statement of conscience against chattel slavery is discoverable. Slavery was just part of reality; the way things are. In the 19th Century slavery was abolished and in the 21st Century, that slavery is abominable is a universal dogma. From earliest civilisation it was about 9,000 years until it was abolished by a budgerigar event.

Late in the 17th Century the first private monopoly of creating and owning all of a nation's money was achieved with the establishment of the Bank of England. Never again would anybody but the government-chartered-money-creating banks own any money in the fullest sense. We would just rent it from the banking system for a rental called interest. By getting some of this rented money we could think that we owned it, but we didn't really, because as a nation and as a people, on balance, we had nothing. Every dollar was born and remained in existence, as a debt.

There are two ways of doing this. If more money is needed in society we can create it, which is done very cheaply, and share it around equally. Alternately we can have the banks create the same amount and increase our indebtedness every year. This we do.

While most of us spend most of our waking hours on earth in money seeking activity, we won't consider taking our share of the new money creations. Is this mental laziness, or the conviction that if other people aren't saying that they want it, then I don't want it? After all, am I my brother's budgerigar?

By acknowledging our collective irrationality, our often seemingly randomly arrived at opinions, out weakness for compliance with the accepted view, our susceptibility to group thinking and our mental laziness in pursuing the real truth which is often at variance with human thinking, we may if we persist, create a society which is more aware of its limitations in these respects, and be able to deliver greater efficiency in terms of human satisfaction.

Perhaps the implications are that we might walk humbly, peaceably, intelligently, and best watch that the ways of the budgerigars do not overtake and misdirect us into folly.

An Eternally Triumphant Mystery?

S peculative thought in the West seems to have been inaugurated by an ancient Greek called Thales. His hypothesis that all matter was composed of water was disputed with antithesis galore, and the current synthesis of particles is no less challenged. Perhaps it is time for another very problematic conjecture like Thales'; "The human organism is controlled and directed through politics".

We may start this exploration with a story; a story told by Dr Kitty Little, an Oxford University academic, in her Memorandum submitted in October 1978 to the Royal Commission on Criminal Organisations in the UK.

Best to quote it: "*I first became aware of some of the problems that could be posed by infiltration .... when I attended a meeting in University College, Oxford, in October 1940 ... the leader of its political section, who spoke at that meeting, explained that it* (the organisation in question) *had not been given a name, and was not to be given a name, because without a name it would be more difficult to prove that it was a definite organisation.*

"Despite this superficial vagueness we were given a precise account of the subversive structure. It was in three main sections, the political, economic and biological, together with a smokescreen of fringe left-wing organisations ... that was to help conceal the existence of the three inner groups. The membership and structure of

these three inner groups was definite, with the head of the biological section the overall head of the organisation."

The questions and implications arising from the above quote are profoundly challenging. The predominance of the biological is implicit. The subservience of the political to the economic and biological is also implicit.

Politics is, in essence, the scramble to create law and impose it on the human organism. Economics is in command of all of the elements dictating to politics; the media through ownership and mortgages, academia through sponsorship and patronage and fear of "bad press", and other education through the Universities' think tanks, industry through acquisition and debt, and so forth.

Socialists are trained from birth to believe that property is the basis of economic control. It is not. All property is acquired with, and directed through, money. Money is something completely different to property. Money is a claim on property, which people will accept because of its claim upon the property of others.

Property does not create any money. All money is created by the Chartered Banks which all Governments have been induced to authorise to create money. The cost of actually creating money from nothing is approximately nothing. The cost of acquiring it from others demands offering equivalent value.

When all that money will buy is available to those who create all the money that there is, thereby largely determining the political agenda, we are left with vain and avaricious politicians in a very small and crowded room, each pridefully reassuring the others of his or her own importance.

While the intellectually lazy have always easily assumed that Governments "run the country", the natural aristocrats who will invest in thought have readily enough seen otherwise. Well then, does economics control and direct the human organism?

If by economics one means property, the answer is no. If the *ownership of property* is what is meant as the agent of control, we are not much closer. Ownership is tentative, and conditional upon servicing its upkeep and maintenance, and paying its taxes. Money acquires property, and is also what enables it to be kept. As the sanction in economics, when rendered down, is the ability to create a society's money at no cost, it then must control all the "art", in what is described as "the art of the possible".

So the idea that politics is of primary importance must be put aside.

So how is it that in Kitty Little's account, the biological is accorded primacy?

I really have no opinion as to the veracity of anything that Kitty Little might say. Being probably at least twenty years old when she attended the meeting in 1940, neither she nor her contemporaries are likely to be around to interview. The fact that she may have been either truthful or an hallucinating psychopath, is with her, as it was with Thales, immaterial. She has raised up a question.

This is a mystery and it is way outside of the range of considerations for all but one in a thousand of the population, just now. Let's begin by walking around it and kicking the tyres.

"Control of the human organism" involves the control of its component parts, who are called persons. It seems axiomatic that a knowledge of what we are trying to influence might take precedence over arranging the means whereby it is done. Even so, this would be meaningless if no method of achieving control could be suggested and given effect.

Here we are back into Thales country; posing questions and making outrageous suggestions.

If I am told that the moon is made of blue-vein cheese, I will not believe it. Why? Most likely because I know what blue-vein cheese is. If on the other hand I am told that it is made of eseehc niev-eulb (the same spelled backwards) I would probably find this plausible if say, four scientists would just prostitute themselves into giving it plausibility in return for research grants. As George Bernard Shaw is reputed to have said: "That which is not readily understood is taken to be profound."

That lies are best believed when one is intimidated by a lack of understanding, is, after all, as axiomatic as saying that tomatoes should be eaten with salt. We are controlled by our ideas of what is true. The truth only has suasion if given credence. Lies though, if given credence assume all the properties of the truth (in our minds at least), and being infinite in number and like monies, being costlessly created, they offer higher dividends perhaps, to spin-doctors with a knowledge of our biological propensities.

After all, if politics is the art of the possible, what is possible, at least theoretically, is close to infinite if only lies can be made to be believed. Here we are not discussing lies which are baldly stated of course, but those which are intimated, implied, or attributed to others with standing or prestige, or statements made without discussion or dissent which are usually adjudged to be true.

Perhaps the ascendency of biological knowledge over its lower levels, is that while politicians and economists have enormous vocabularies of lies, and energy and tenacity in telling them, and exhibit Herculean endurance in persisting in them; in the end, which lies will be believed is more important to know than is their production statistics. Perhaps this is why alongside measurements of GDP we do not measure GDL (Gross Domestic Lying).

Having kicked one tyre, perhaps it is time to kick another?

It seems that we all wish to aspire to something. We need to. We confer prestige on persons or institutions, and in some measure offer obeisance to these recipients. Our deference is given in honour of ourselves, as we are at least the spiritual appointees of the esteemed.

After lies, perhaps betrayal may offer the greatest dividends in controlling society. After all, if society is simply doing what comes naturally, then nobody in particular is controlling it at all. Nobody has ever been betrayed except by someone to whom they had given trust. So the biological leadership must have knowledge of how to win trust and best exploit it, or at least use it.

Perhaps a third tyre now.

Biology tells us that birds of a feather flock together. If the objective is to enhance the coherence, goodwill and strength of a targeted society, then homogeneity is a most effective policy. The encouragement of throwing together peoples of dissimilar "feathers", be they religious, ethnic or class considerations, will bring increasing disharmony if that is the object. Constant reassurances to the contrary will delay the friction if one's intent is to magnify it.

The above three considerations might be nominated as credulousness, deference and identity (the harmony/disharmony above). Their significance, use and
efficacy are in the province of the biological.

There is another area of influence, and this one is very little examined. This
influence is usually described as subliminal. It involves methods of communicating with our subconscious minds without arousing the attention of our
conscious one. Its methods include words in songs sung backwards or at
different frequencies, and images in films or videos of only 1/10 of a second
or less which the conscious mind cannot see. The ice cubes in Gilbey's Gin
advertisements spelling "sex", and the earliest glass coke bottles being designed
to suggest curvaceous women, are examples.

At least twenty years before I started writing essays I saw a report which I
cannot now rediscover. It experimented with subliminal advertising at movie
theatres. They inserted subliminal urging in the slides shown for a confec-
tionery, a drink, or popcorn alternately on different nights, and then counted
sales during the intervals. As the audience changed every night the influence
from one night did not linger to the next. Sales followed the subliminal advertising, rising according to what had been advertised.

The advertising industry is pretty canny about pronouncing on the effectiveness of such advertisements. They not only produce them, they retain in
confidence all of the data upon sales responses to them. As they are supposed
to be commercially driven, why do they persist with them in the face of their
ineffectiveness?

If the subconscious mind is ahead of our conscious ones in cognition, then
how far is it in advance of our knowing it? If an image duration of one thou-
sandth of a second were inserted 100 times in a visual presentation, it may be
completely beyond discovery, though effective. Could a message comprised of
every 3rd or 7th word in a text be discerned by the subconscious and influence us
unbeknown?

Who has the resources to properly and fully research this? A science of the
biological predispositions of the sub-consciousness of mankind fully funded by

a monopoly of creating society's money could do it. Is there another candidate available?

An eternal mystery for mankind is ourselves. How do we discover what we are incapable of recognising, if there is any such, when by definition recognising it is unavailable to us?

The Greeks were wrong about earth, water, fire and air. Is it really all a matter of another four; credulousness, deference, identity and subliminal suggestion?

Yes, there is an eternally triumphant mystery as to the sources of collective human motivations, though given our dearth of self-knowledge, and our disinclination through pride to accept this, will *what* it is, and *where* it is, forever have to remain *as* it is?

Every mystery story is expected to end with its explanation. We are only comfortable with mysteries when there aren't any left. We are usually angered when we have persisted right to the end of a story, only to find that the mystery is not answered for us.

It is a bit like chaos theory which tells us that a butterfly flapping its wings in the Amazon can alter the course of hurricanes. What is the good of that, if you don't tell us which butterfly on what twig, and name the tree? Its importance, actually, is primary!

The first and most important thing to know about a mystery is that there is one, and the second thing is an idea of where it is. The most important thing that this does, on the other hand, is to sensitise us to listen more carefully to ourselves, which is the only place which offers any prospect that it may be discovered.

Furthermore and moreover, might there not be a *"fifth man"* in the background of this mystery?

CULPABILITY?

You don't have to actually rob a bank to be culpable for the robbery. If it was done with your knowing assistance in any way, you are culpable. You may have only loaned the getaway car, or provided details of the security surveillance, or advised who of the staff was the most readily intimidated, but this establishes your guilt.

If you are complicit in a crime (have complied with its execution in some way), your guilt and culpability is established.

The reach of culpability is the subject of this essay. Where does the tacit complicity in committing, aiding, or enabling a crime end?

Sometimes the fact of a crime is indisputable, though its nature is less clear.

The felling of the Twin Towers in the so-called 9-11 event in 2001 is probably the best-known crime of the 21st Century, though its exact nature is less clear.

The insurmountable problem with the conventional explanation of this crime comes down to physics. A brick will fall through a vacuum at an acceleration rate of 9.8 metres per second per second. It falls through air a little slower as air gives some resistance, and through water at only half this speed. Bricks fall through steel reinforced concrete yet more slowly again.

In this case a concrete and steel building which had held up the top 20% of the structure for decades, in a single moment of time, lost all its strength and resistance. This was so much so that it fell down in free-fall time; at the same rate as though there was only air beneath it. Physical science does not say that this is impossible, but it has thus far only been able to suggest one possibility for it happening. That explanation is professional and well executed demolition.

No alternate explanation in keeping with the laws of physics has yet been made. The problem for most is that this raises more questions than it answers. We can deal with some of them.

Who could possibly have set the explosive charges that appeared to be crackling as the buildings fell? Nobody could believe that they were set by Americans. They could never be kept from talking. Could a disciplined body of foreign nationals have been brought in, done the wiring and returned home before the event? Most people can think of at least two nations who could do this if they wished it.

But how could this have been done when nobody noticed? It wasn't. A large body of technicians were observed "renovating the lifts" for weeks before 9-11.

But the Government would never agree to something like this! I think that is probably true, but after it was done, things would change. A Government could survive a surprise attack by hostile fanatics as the crashing aeroplanes evidenced. Could it survive a deliberate demolition killing thousands which could not be blamed on terrorists? Certainly not!

Whoever wired the Twin Towers was perfectly safe from the Government pursuing this issue. The rage would have torn down every brick of the political edifice and the ultimate fallout would have been utterly unknowable.

Of course, there is more. How come the organisers of the demolition knew that the "Arabs" would hijack some planes and give perfect plausibility to the envisaged future programme of retaliation? "Nursing" hostile plots is a standard secret intelligence practice which goes right back to the time of Mary Queen of Scots, and beyond. Every discovered plot is first assessed by professional intelligence, as to whether it can be bounced back against the perpetrators.

All the elaborations above make it difficult for us to accept the obvious; that the Twin Towers were detonated. Yes, it is very difficult, and this is very understandable. Does this excuse the acceptance of the impossible? The social pressure against accepting a very great elaboration of deceit is most formidable. Somebody somewhere would have had to associate with others to make it happen this way. Conspiracy? Alas! Perish the thought!

So, twenty years of war followed. Libya, Syria, Yemen, Iraq and Afghanistan were torn apart, economies were destroyed, tens of thousands killed, hundreds of thousands made homeless refugees, and over $10 trillion flowed into the coffers of the industrial military complexes.

In the end all this was only possible with the assistance and compliance of the culpable.

More than ten thousand engineers and architects signed written statements that the lack of resistance of the concrete buildings at the Twin Towers was impossible, other than through deliberate demolition. Building number 7 which was a few hundred metres from the Twin Towers, and was not hit by an aeroplane, also "fell down" that day. None have any other plausible explanation, so who is complicit and who is culpable?

Guilt clearly falls upon a number of parties to this demolition event. Those who lay the demolition charges, those who ordered and paid for them, those who maintained silence about this, the terrorists who hijacked the planes, and those who saw and assisted them in order to excuse the demolition, are clearly guilty.

When all these and other guilty ones are identified, what then?

The twenty years of war which followed was still only possible because of one factor. Several hundred million people chose to believe a lie, and an obvious one at that. I am told that ignorance is no defence in the eyes of the law, though this certainly seems rather harsh to me. Still, the mad American adventures in the Middle East which continued for 20 years were all built upon the propensity of a large public to believe a lie.

The religious have always held that what we believe will take us either to paradise or to hell. It does seem to be so.

Yet why was the lie so attractive, so seductive, so beguiling? The final answer is probably cowardice. The acceptance of this one lie enabled compliance with the sung narrative of the Government, and the media, and therefore almost everyone. A comfortable life in which we all agree, and at no cost, except to others, is attractive.

This cowardice in the face of censure for non-compliance is an ancient factor in politics.

The United States declared war on Spain when the Spaniards sank the battleship USS Maine in Havana Harbour in April 1898. The indignation and outrage were fierce, and the US seized the Philippines and Puerto Rico in retaliation. A century later the Maine was raised to reveal the blast was from the inside out. No apologies were made.

Guy Fawkes was apprehended for trying to blow up Parliament House in 1605 with gun powder. As the manufacture of gunpowder at the time was a government monopoly, where did it come from? The poor simple minded Catholic zealots were duped, and the persecution of Catholics was enabled for decades. The majority of the English were still Catholic at the time of Guy Fawkes, but not afterwards as it was unpatriotic.

Lies are very common and popular in politics. They often come in great clusters to explain complexity. This is usually their undoing. For example, a fraudulent "Hitler's Diary" being sold to the Spiegel magazine for a large fortune was undone, when one person was reported as being in Berlin on a day when he was really in Paris.

The evidence for global warming is everywhere reported and supported. Modelling testifying to it is taken as being "beyond questioning" and indisputable. That global warming and climate change is a fact, does however, have its problems.

Its largest problem comes from the science of geology. Geology studies the formation of rocks and the conditions existent when they were formed. They tell the climate alarmists the most inconvenient things, so of course the climate alarmists don't listen. Here is a sample:

There are 400 parts per million of CO^2 in the atmosphere now. In the Cambrian period 530 million years ago, the most prolific period ever in producing new life forms, the CO^2 ppm were 2,200 and the temperature was only 3.5 degrees Centigrade warmer. Ninety million years later in the Paleozoic period there were 2,100 ppm of CO^2, and the world was in an ice age and colder than it is now. 250 million years ago in the Permian period when CO^2 was at just 500 ppm, the world was four degrees C warmer than now. Geologically there is no close correlation to be found between CO^2 and temperature: see https://www.dr-robert-fagan.com/#:~:text=Dr%20Fagan%20developed%20a %20particular,undergraduate%20and%20post%2Dgraduate%20levels How can this be if it is a greenhouse gas?

CO^2 is very effective as a greenhouse gas, but only in intercepting infrared radiation in very limited wavelengths. It is most effective at infrared's specific wavelengths of 4.102 and 15.589 microns. Either side of these lengths its effectiveness diminishes and is nonexistent at 0.5 microns away. This means that CO^2 does not act as a greenhouse gas at all outside of the infrared wavelengths from 3.6 to 4.6 microns, and from 15.1 to 16.1 microns.

Water vapour is also an effective greenhouse gas in these wavelength bands, so even at 400 ppm most of the work that it may do in these narrow windows is already done, and the atmosphere is three degrees C warmer than if there were no CO^2. Double the ppm to 800 and it can only give about another 0.3 degrees of warming. Double it again to 1,600 ppm and less than another 0.3 degrees is achieved.[1]

Heating the world's atmosphere significantly more with CO^2 is not possible, but superheating public paranoia with it is an everyday occurrence. Vested interests which want to build wind turbines, solar arrays and electric cars, or outlaw coal and make electricity expensive have "skin in this game". But the public do not?

Essentially the public does not want to bother its pretty little head with any truths, which if accepted, would put them at variance with the sung narrative of convention, which is a supposed majority. They prefer lies to the bother which the truth invariably brings. One can hardly be condemnatory about it. It is such an innocuous sin. All it does is hand the thinking and the running of the world

---

1. For a full explanation of the limitations of CO2 see https://www.youtub e.com/watch?v=57pU2F-bIQs

over to elites, and this by people who would insist that they are democrats. In a sense the elites are perfectly entitled to exploit their advantage, as they alone (or pretty much) have given it attention. They understand the public's weakness and vulnerability, the public itself does not. Nevertheless, in the distortions resulting from the global alarmists' sung narrative, most people are culpable. Believing a lie gives it life.

Lies in public policy areas such as health (pandemics) and the environment (that corals are growing fastest and best in the warmest waters is demonstrably true, while most believe that global warming is killing the ones in the coolest water) come to mind. Finance also has its policy forming fallacies and provides an example with which to end this essay.

If it is true that believing a lie makes us culpable for many a wrongdoing, disbelieving a truth is perhaps worthy of even greater condemnation. There is, for this reason, no escape in cynicism where nothing is believed. If you get either your "believing" or your "disbelieving" wrong, you are culpable. Humanity is forever trapped in a morass of responsibility. The best policy is probably to enjoy it.

Most people refuse to believe that money is all created (no, not earned, but created) at practically no cost, by private interests who retain its ownership, and only ever rent it to society for a charge called interest. Society only ever has an amount of money equal to what it owes to the banking system which creates it. The only money we have, is what we have had secondhand from those who borrowed it from the banks, to which they still owe it.[2]

Of course, if all money is created at no cost and retained by private interests, the hope of denying them anything which money can buy is illusory. All that can be bought, persuaded, cajoled, tempted, or subdued with money is theirs at no cost to themselves. Are the media, public education and government itself

---

2. The truth and explanation of money creation which is created privately and held in cyberspace is widely available. The author's work Different Essays available from Balboa Publications through the internet has many explanatory pieces on money creation.

invulnerable to the many wiles of money? Government budgets do not contain revenue from money creation; it is all taxed or borrowed.

That there is One Ring of Power in the world to Rule Them All, is too commanding of our lazy selves to do something about it, or to allow us to dare to believe it. This is why J R R Tolkien had to tell us the truth in fantasy. We could have no interest in Tolkien's Middle Earth unless there was One Ring of Power to draw and bind them, but we can't endure the truth of a commanding central influence in our own world. Hell, that would mean that every poor bastard would have to become a Frodo!

FARMING PEOPLE

U ntil about ten to twelve thousand years ago, it is thought that there was no farming at all. Hunting and gathering sustained the small populations of the time.

As a farmer myself I suspect that animals were the first to be domesticated. Herbivores which could be caught young, hobbled, and tamed offered an easier option with less genetic change being necessary than with many plants. Both plants and animals were domesticated long ago, though modifications to their genetics and husbandry continues unabated to this day.

Exploiting natural things to enhance our economy had been our major preoccupation for millennia. It used to be the endeavour at the cutting edge of improving our lot, and the vast majority of people were employed in it. By 1900 however, only 40% of the population were living and working on farms in countries like the United States and Australia. Then came the last great reform in farming.

It came with the internal combustion engine in the form of a tractor and led to changes so revolutionary that a hundred years later, farming only occupied one to two percent of the population. Human effort as the dominant resource required in producing food and fibre was over. Another farming revolution, perhaps more significant, also began from about the year 1900. As farming plants and animals became an accomplished art, another form of farming was taken up. This one farmed people themselves.

In the long learning curve of domesticating animals, we learned a lot about them, and we probably learned even more about ourselves. A key thing in controlling animals was to be understood in observing their reactions to provocation. These reactions come in two types. One was to put as much distance as possible between the predator and themselves. The other was to put as many of their friends as possible between the predator and themselves.

I observed a herd of cattle with the first approach in North Queensland in the 1970s. Six very experienced and accomplished stockmen ("ringers") attempted to drive 400 head into nearby cattle yards. The herd immediately scattered with urgency and only six head were captured by the men throwing down a beast each and tying it up. The greater mob were later yarded with the aid of helicopters and by trapping them at watering points.

The policy of avoidance preferred and encouraged by farmers is the second. This does not involve diverse flight, but rather, the animal placing itself on the opposite side of the herd to the predator in the expectation that it will eat someone else instead. This is typified in a tight ball of sardines under predation, and herds and flocks holding together. An exploding star has too many fragments to allow many to be caught. A flock or herd continually adjusting itself away from threat whilst maintaining its "safety in numbers" policy, is easily directed into enclosures in its entirety. When farming people this must be borne in mind.

Being a more rational being, shock and fear is best induced if humans are to be encouraged into the "safety in numbers" mode of defending themselves. The age of experimenting with farming people opened in earnest with the first World War. That men would act with bravery (brazenly risk death) rather than face the censure of their "mob" has been understood from earliest warfare. It was a high art form in 1914-18.

A number of experiments with farming human beings will be considered with a view to understanding the basic elements needed. Shock and fear need to be present to induce the psychosis conducive of hiding from the danger behind others. In the first experiment to be considered, the Bolshevik revolution of

1917, the shock was provided by the massive mismanagement and disastrous Russian defeats of World War I.

Once fear is present, all that is necessary to establish hegemony is to be found in showing that all others think in a given and prescribed way. With the right means this can be artificially attained, and rationality is then deliberately though subconsciously abandoned, to avoid one being singled out. As will be seen, rationality will not be allowed to interrupt the security to be enjoyed through uniform thought with the "herd".

The Bolsheviks were a minority of only 40,000 in a population of over 100 million. No matter, they took control of the means of telling the people what the people thought. Trotsky brought five million dollars in gold from New York, Stalin had robbed many banks, and by this and concentrating themselves in St Petersburg, the media of the day (the newspapers) were brought under their control. What everybody thought that everybody thought, was soon - in the primordial inevitability of herd conformity - self-fulfilled. Once settled and accepted under stress, only decades of pain and disappointment can undo such surety, and that only in a later generation.

The next great experiment in farming people came in Germany in the 1930s. The shock and stress of the war was compounded by the vindictive peace imposed by the victors. All that was necessary now for social control was a monopoly of informing the people what the people thought, and then, always wanting to believe what most others were believed to believe, they also believed it, and therefore it was so. But surely this is irrational? Exactly! It was in accord with the human propensity to conform with the herd, and was never, once adopted, open to any logical exposition of the truth. This would have been an "inhuman response", (though one which none ever claims as being so), which made it unrecognisable and therefore unaddressed.

The experiments continued with knowledge of how best to farm people being progressively improved. A more recent example of threat, with herd-think prevailing over logic, was provided by the Covid pandemic of 2021.

A group was told and accepted that 80% of the population at that time was vaccinated. The Government reported that 80% of those infected that day were vaccinated and that 20% were not, and that those committed to hospital were also 80% vaccinated and that 20% were not. Whether correct or otherwise, no one in the group disputed these figures.

It was then suggested that this meant that vaccination was ineffective in preventing infection, and also, that it didn't lessen the severity of infection once contracted. Not one person in the group would accept this, including even those with university training in interpreting statistics. Mathematical certainty could not prevail over these people's commitment to the group-thought of the time.

People, like sardines, once they are swirling in a meatball under perceived threat, are completely impervious to any factual observation offered. Contradiction of "herd-think" is itself a threat to perceptions of security, and man is pathologically incapable of accepting it. This is not new. It has been a fixed part of the instinctive behaviour of humans no less than that of sardines, and herds, and flocks from the beginning of time. We are an irrational being, and an obstinate, determined and wilful one when herd-thinking is threatened with disturbance.

If 20% of a certain population were red headed, but their average athletic ability, mathematical scores, or susceptibility to some diseases were identical with the 80%, then it is an inescapable conclusion that red hairiness is irrelevant in such cases. Only committed herd-thinking that it be otherwise can deny this logic; and of course, it does, because it is older and more deeply entrenched in our emotional/thought patterns than any rationality. Examples of slavish herd-think abound.

Fear of "global warming", and media unanimity that it is caused by human action releasing CO^2 into the atmosphere, has produced a type of carbon-phobia. Most are convinced that increased CO^2 has the ability to vastly increase temperatures, and that science confirms this. Actually, science says that a significant temperature increase from rising CO^2 levels is impossible.

Professor of Physics at Loyola Marymount University, Michel Van Biezen, explained this in one of his many videos available at https://www.youtube.c om/watch?v=57pU2F-bIQs on the 4th of June, 2015. CO^2, while efficient as a greenhouse gas, only operates at two very limited infrared wavelengths, these being in the vicinity of 4.1 and 15.6 microns. Only 18% of the heat (infrared radiation) departing earth is in these wavelengths. Water vapour already intercepts over 70% of this, being a much more significant greenhouse gas than CO^2, so only 5% of the heat escaping earth can be intercepted by CO^2 whatever its concentration. At 400 parts per million most of this 5% is already captured.

This explains why in the Cambrian Period when CO^2 was at 2,000 ppm it was very little warmer, though the earth was much greener because of carbon dioxide's benefit to plants.

When the media cooperates in farming public opinion, to the point that each is convinced that all others think in some specific way, human thought swirls around in the fear of exiting consensus. Nothing can induce it to leave the safety of "unified-thought"; not science, not reason, nor any evidence whatsoever. Human thought, like the sardines in a spherical meatball, will not leave it. Telling of the limitations of CO^2 can never be heard, and is pathologically impossible to any minds which have not been prepared to resist their thought being farmed.

Fear and the media's consensus have convinced the world that the Twin Towers fell down because two planes flew into them. More than ten thousand engineers and architects have pointed out, and signed declarations, that without deliberate modern demolition the buildings could never instantaneously lose all resistance to gravity as they did. There was never even a remote prospect for years afterwards that the majority could hear such as this. Why? Because we are primordial organic beings and must act like it.

In May 2020 we all saw George Floyd being held down and asphyxiated. He told us in a loud voice about sixty times that he couldn't breathe. Nobody else has ever been able to yell it even four times without another breath. In emotional circumstances and with no media dissent, we will all believe the impossible and resent any who mention it.

More examples are superfluous, as men in their "sardinian meatballs" and placing others between themselves and their fears, cannot allow any thought to enter.

These few observations are the specifics upon which the science of farming populations is based. Advertising is in full flight in exploiting mass psychology. People-farming goes further, as advertising only urges certain actions upon us, while "PF", through fear and the media's unanimous repetition, seeks to overrule alternate thought. It is still early days in this art, but it is developing nicely, and will in all probability define the future of the human organism.

There is no hope in seeking to change human nature or wishing it were otherwise. We must accept our propensity to be farmed if we are not to be farmed. Those outside of the spinning spherical meatball of human herd-thought are their brothers' keepers. Their help will be resented, disputed, and refused, but they cannot allow themselves to be inhibited. Men and mankind have a common destiny.

Of course, an aspect of intelligent domestication of animals thus far unexamined, is the inducement that can be offered with food. Food offerings to the local bird populations will progressively tame them. In time they trust the farmer and conform to what is necessary to get it. Food is too abundantly available to humans to sufficiently influence their behaviour. Money plays the part, in domesticating humans into the service of others, that food does with animals.

No modern money is created by private persons through counterfeiting, and no money being created forms revenue in any Government budget. All money is created and owned by our banking systems; usually private systems. Two inevitabilities arise from this. One is that all media will be owned by, or mortgaged or beholden to the money-creating entities. The second is that no media will ever tell us this, so few will have the "bottle" to believe that the private right to create money and use it to control society exists, as herd-think will not affirm it.

Those who watch the domestication of their fellows with continual assurances in the media that CO^2 can significantly heat the planet, that vaccinations are effective in preventing the number or severity of covid-19 infections, or that buildings sometimes instantaneously lose their resistance to gravity, have insufficient media to contradict it. The volume of repetition is the determinant of public thinking, not truth or logic when they are unexpressed sufficiently.

I don't think that the elites necessarily have any specific nasty intent towards us at the moment; they are just practicing with the idea that farming people will come in handy sometime. So, what is to be done?

The first thing is to accept our credulity in the face of herd-think. The next thing is to accept that a seeming conformity in thought can be artificially arranged by a dominant media. Acceptance of these raises awareness, and the media's repertoire of sung narratives repeated too often is thus open to, and will invoke, the necessary suspicion. This is a beginning.

It cannot be ended of course while society allows elite interests to create, own, and distribute as debt, all of the money existent. Whether we can be farmed into a state of permanent and unrecognised submission, with the media as Pied Piper ever playing a one-think melody, is likely to be the one significant and important question for the human organism until it is decided one way or the other.

Perhaps if we just know that farming humans is happening, it may be enough to end it. *It will never be an open question being discussed until it has already been destroyed.* If this is so, and the media is silent, its existence is then affirmed, is it not? Take care.

TALKING WITH CROWDS

A dvice to men about their relationships typically appertains to a woman, God, or their associates at work. What really shifts men's opinions, ideas, aptitudes, and convictions is usually how they relate to the "herd", or if you will, the "mob" or the "collective" of which they regard themselves as a part.

Research is increasingly telling us, it seems, that the opinions we adopt, the ideas we accept and the policies we opt for, are what we think "others" will concur in.

The global advertising industry annually spends hundreds of billions upon influencing us.

They spend many more again in assessing whether it worked, and why.

Approximately, it works like this. In deciding what we make of a proposition such as "CO^2 is threatening the climate" we don't usually consult our independent conclusions in the matter. This is because few of us have them. It is far too expensive in time and opportunity to explore many abstract academic propositions. What actually happens is that we "pick up" or absorb what majority opinion appears to be. When we are asked to take a position on this question, our subconscious mind which loves us, intervenes saying, *stay with the mob and the safety of numbers*. The perceived majority opinion is adopted on the basis of its "safety".

This is probably the most significant and widely employed strategy in controlling nature. It is as effective amongst animals as it is with humans.

In mustering widely dispersed cattle on an open plain into captivity, this strategy is subtly employed. Drifting well out from the outermost cattle, one attempts with minimum pressure to induce them to move a little closer to the others. This continues at the most leisurely pace practicable. As the cattle come into closer contact with each other their awareness of each other increases. In time they progressively look to the others to suggest their own response.

A small nudge on one side of the mob can change their direction of movement a little. Offering the mildest threat causes a movement towards the centre of the mob, and the mob readjusts slightly. The principle here is that if the crocodile is to eat one of us, it should always be someone else. By inducing the mob of cattle to always take the safety option, in time they are all herded into the cattle yards and every single one is shipped off to the abattoir. The crocodile can eat them all because they prefer the others to be eaten first.

Those which stand out from the swirling ball of sardines are first eaten when the tuna and dolphins are herding them. In time of course all are eaten, unless the predators' appetites prove insufficient for the task.

Are men so dissimilar? My brother once spent many hours in discussions with professional army officers recounting their experiences. They spoke of a training exercise in which, at a point when the men were crawling under obstacles, live ammunition was fired over their heads. When the recruits were drawn from suburbia, they all crawled in closer and closer towards each other. Rural recruits dispersed as much as they could.

Their consciousness of the falsity of "safety in crowds" differentiated their responses.

The dynamics of convincing everyone of what everyone else is thinking is changing radically with the artificiality of "mega media". This in turn, if we are mob sensitive, changes what we will accept as true.

Kipling's poem asks, "*If you can talk with crowds and keep your virtue...*" Implicit in this is that virtue may be threatened. Talking with crowds can hardly be thought to challenge virtue in the sense of sexual misdemeanour or petty pilfering. It offers the altogether greater sin of prostituting our judgement, opinion and intellectual integrity to conform with the perceptions of "others". Ultimately this can mean that we cease to be persons, and become but "outcomes" of advertising campaigns or political propaganda.

The politically and socially correct are piteous outcomes of what they have heard most often and have internalised and adopted at a subhuman level.

The most heinous and demeaning of all human sins comes with surrendering to the popular, and wholly because it is popular with others. In a certain sense we cease to be. When we decide to be what everyone else seems to be, we can retain nothing of ourselves.

What all this seems to mean is that when something without an objective truth is widely held to be true, it must be treated with the utmost suspicion. It has very probably been induced into the popular mind by a vested interest with the means of endless repetition and at the very least, whether this is so or no, this forms the primary duty of care of a functioning human being who takes responsibility for himself.

We must examine the pedigree of every idea to know its agenda in society's sung narrative. Who benefits is, as ever, the question.

So What's it About?

There are myriad misconceptions and misunderstandings abroad about what Social Credit and the Movement of that name are about.

Social Credit has technical aspects, especially with respect to finance.

It has a clear and well defined philosophy, not in the classical sense of engagement and contention with such figures as Plato, Hegel, Kant and such, but rather in the sense that philosophy is defined and pursued as "an exploration and exposition of the nature of truth", especially as it appertains to efficiency in the attainment of human satisfaction in social endeavour.

Its ultimate objectives are social, having to do with satisfactory organisation and relationships for society in delivering a free, responsible and creative society best suited to the self-development of persons in areas economic, social and spiritual.

The above has no relationship with the system of social surveillance and oppression which the Chinese have chosen to name "social credit". This system is both antisocial and discreditable; an example of Marxist double-speak which is best described as Orwellian.

The most popular misunderstanding of Social Credit is that it has to do with contention in respect to money creation, usury, a public deficiency of purchasing power, debt, proposing a national dividend, and of course something known as the A + B theorem. While the Movement deals with all these things, they are necessarily given attention only as the means towards what the Movement is about.

When asked whether the Movement is about "life, the universe and everything" the only correct answer is "No, it is strictly about life and everything".

The misunderstanding is somewhat in the nature of confusing sanctions with the reason that they are employed. The Roman Empire marched legions hither and yon to assert its hegemony. If flying paper kites would have served the object as well, there would have not been any legions. As it was, the military was the key sanction, the one of primary importance, and that is why the legions marched and the world fell in behind them.

No longer do soldiers of flesh and blood with weapons of bronze and steel command. Today the sanctions which matter come in their billions. They say to the media "Come" and it comes, to the university academics "Sit" or "Stay" and they comply, and to industry "Go" and it does. These legions march through balance sheets, through telecommunications, through board meetings and take easy command of the best lawyers, businessmen and crowd psychologists.

These billions have none of the weaknesses of flesh and blood. Indeed, they have neither. These are much more formidable; for they are enumerated abstractions. They exist only as recorded numbers, either as magnetic blips in computers or ink smudges upon paper accounts or notes.

The soldiers of bone, blood and sinew are prostrate before the stronger force, which is of no fixed form or matter whatever. Then what empowers money to rule?

The simplest of things. We covet it. The reason that we covet it is even more remarkable. We only have use for it and want it because others want it, and they want it only for the same reason. Whether what we all want is gold, bottle tops or blips recording bank deposits is immaterial, if there is a sufficiency of covetousness associated with it, it will and does serve as our money supply.

Yet this of itself is not really the difficulty. The whole thing is awkward because the creation of money (not value) is a private monopoly. Changing it into a public monopoly would probably make it worse. When the legions of money-billions are brought into existence from a central point or coterie, theirs is the control of their direction, and the human organism is directed (read enslaved) to the full measure that society will obey money.

Society metamorphosing into the form most favourable to the "Golden Internationale" is the current norm. This "entity", the loosely associated banking houses across the world which create our money and rent it out, and continue therefore to own monies equal to all of it, now stand to inherit the earth.

Unfortunately, being just like us, they tend to act in their own self-interest, though their self-interest is unrecognisably different from ours. People who "have everything" don't exist, except in the imaginations of the poor. Those who have more than we can imagine having, do exist, but in common with the rest of the human race there is something else they always need. It can be described in one word; what they want is *more*.

Privilege tends to protect itself. The privilege of creating a society's money is a societal privilege. Defending it involves influencing society itself. This places their self-interest on a plain which is beyond the focus of almost all persons.

In an estimation made in the 1980s by Cardinal Wyszyński and his protégé the later Pope John Paul II, and since the demise of the Soviet Union, there are now only two contenders vying for the future direction of the human organism. These are of course the Golden Internationale with the sanctions of all that money will buy, and the Church, which attends to, and is interested in, what it won't.

The principle irreconcilable contention as to the best societal construction to be had, and of which most people have never heard, is subsidiarity. This principle of the Church's social teaching holds that no level of governance should be exercised at any level which a lower level is quite capable of properly exercising. The State should not appropriate the functions of the family where the family can responsibly fulfil that role. A World Government should not assume the function of filling the potholes in our roads from local governments.

The Golden Internationale does not subscribe to subsidiarity. Its application would prejudice their hegemony. This struggle, which operates above the conscious scrutiny of most of us, enervates the policy of the higher functionaries which command the private right to create and own money creations.

Disabling the party which holds for subsidiarity, the Church, involves disparaging traditional values, and undoing adherence to those values and teachings which have informed the West from its birth. The decks have to be cleared of such which inhibit the achievement of that utopia born of the will-to-power.

If the Church opposes the practicing of homosexuality, gender confusion, euthanasia, and the elevation of the functions of governance to places above individual initiative, then such are to be advocated, encouraged and "normalised". And this of course, not because the Golden Internationale favours the immoral, necessarily, but because this is of the essence in depreciating the standing of the one cogent force for subsidiarity.

The Golden Internationale is not conspiring, as their charge of denigration against conspiracy theory holds, but logically following the pursuit of their self-interest where it takes them. Its description is merely a matter of semantics. Describe it as you will, if you please.

The interests of the Social Credit Movement are inseparable and at one with those supportive of subsidiarity. There is after all, no other basis upon which freedom can be sustained.

The democratisation of money creations, where additions to the money supply for the purposes of enabling consumption (though not production) are all dispersed to individual proper persons as a National Dividend or otherwise for their benefit, will not be had where the will-to-power is ascendant. An organic culture which builds society up from the individual cannot be attained in the presence of a monopoly of credit creations by elites.

So.... *Social Credit is about efficiency in terms of human satisfaction.*

This necessitates, among other things, an economy so organised as to deliver the economic means of sustaining ourselves with a minimum of labour and other resources. No, the economy is not about jobs and growth, but about freeing us for higher cultural activities in the interests of our self-development.

Social Credit is about life and everything appertaining to having it at its highest level, including economically, culturally and spiritually. The universe, thankfully, remains outside of our jurisdiction.

PART FIVE

Prototype National Accounts – for when politicians want to understand national accounts as thoroughly as directors understand their company's affairs

A Comprehensive Balance Sheet

for the Commonwealth of Australia to 30th June 2020

Assets		**$AUD Billions**
Land		6,185.00
Dwellings		6,531.29
Human resources		
(education and training only)		4,587.30
Non-dwelling constructions		2,965.70
Financial assets with the rest		
of the world		3,069.60
Shares and other equity	1,574.00	
Securities other than shares	811.00	
Loans and placements	366.40	
Other accounts receivable	169.60	
Currency and deposits	121.70	
Monetary gold and		
statutory deposit reserves	12.10	
Insurance technical reserves	14.80	
Sub-soil assets		928.70
Machinery and equipment		668.50
Australian investments abroad		862.10
Consumer durables		412.60
Imports		23.24
Inventory		212.90
Private, non-farm	160.80	
Farm	8.60	
Public authorities	8.30	
Livestock (from Table 60)	25.50	
Plantation standing timber	9.70	
Intellectual property products		247.90
Research and development	100.60	
Mineral and petroleum exploration	92.70	
Computer software	51.20	
Artistic originals	3.40	
Cultivated biological resources		24.50
Weapons systems		75.80
Spectrum availability and allocation		
(communication asset)		20.20
Permission to use natural resources		4.10
Native standing timber		1.70
Goodwill		1.00
Total National Assets		**26,822.13**

Liabilities		**$AUD Billions**
Financial liabilities		
to the rest of the world		3,980.30
Securities other than shares	1,772.10	
Shares and other equity	1,391.20	
Currency and deposits	227.90	
Loans and placements	503.70	
Other accounts payable	75.40	
Monetary gold and		
statutory deposit reserves	6.20	
Insurance technical reserves	3.80	
The Issued Money Supply		2,325.20
Foreign investments in Australia		1,087.90
Exports		31.03
Ownership transfer costs		289.30
Total National Liabilities		**7,713.73**
Net National Assets (Liabilities)		**19,108.40**

Notes to the Account

All statistics have been taken directly from the Australian Bureau of Statistics' tables at https://www.abs.gov.au/statistics/economy/national-accounts/austr alian-system-national-accounts/latest-release#data-download with the following exceptions:

Human Resources (education and training)

Government expenditure on education in 2019-20 was $114.1 billion. See https://www.abs.gov.au/statistics/economy/government/government-finance -statistics-education-australia/latest-release#:~:text=Total%20government%20 education%20expenses%20was,%2441.5%20billio n%20in%202019%2D20

The link https://www.finder.com.au/australian-household-spending-statis tics gives Household Expenditure on education as $55.8 in 2020.

Thus, total spending on education totalled $114.1 plus $55.8 billion to equal $169.9 billion in 2020.

The average working life in Australia is over 40 years, and it may reasonably be considered to be worth its expenditure over 20 years. After 10 years practicing one's craft, we are better bricklayers, accountants, or medicos etc. so there is an experiential appreciation of abilities of perhaps 50%. As we approach retirement there is an actuarial depreciation of the training. A value of our total investment in vocational training might therefore be $169.9 billion x 20 (years of expenditure) x 1.5 to reflect the 50% increase in vocational ability due to experience, and divided by nine tenths to account for provision for retirements.

The result is $4,587.3 billion. In this way both politicians and economists may learn something of our value to each other.

Goodwill

A population which is at peace with each other, possessing common ideas as to the purpose of society, and respected by neighbouring nations as acting in good faith, has a goodwill asset; a gaggle of warring tribes where law is not respected would not. The entry of $1 billion is nominal, and obviously awaits societal attention to national accounts before a realistic figure might be suggested and accepted.

The Issued Money Supply

The link https://fred.stlouisfed.org/series/MABMM301AUM189S gives the money supply (M3) as $2,325.20 billion as at 30th June 2020. If a "current liabilities" figure is required, term deposits which are of course, currently unavailable to the public, should be deducted from this.

Why We Need National Comprehensive Balance Sheets

Balance sheets tell us more than how rich or poor we are. They also tell us why we are rich, or poor, and something about how we managed it.

Knowing how rich we are tells us much about what we can afford. These accounts list all of the advantages (assets) we have in trying to do "stuff", and also list the claims against us (our liabilities) which limit our ability to do things.

If the idea of building a land bridge to Tasmania was suggested, consulting the Balance Sheet would indicate whether we had the wherewithal to do it if we wished.

I have called this balance sheet "comprehensive", not because it is; it doesn't give details of the specifics of the "Machinery and Equipment" for instance, just a total value. It does, however, attempt to surpass the last national balance sheet done by the Australian Bureau of Statistics in 2012, which listed neither one of our greatest assets, nor our greatest liability.

Our greatest asset is of course our people. Just giving the value of our vocational training as we have, shows this, though it is but a small fraction of what has been invested in them.

The greatest claim upon our assets is the issued money supply. While money is a personal asset, at a national level it is like the number of IOUs which have been issued against us, and is a liability. Because politicians often don't understand this, our national interests are often mis-served.

When a farm is sold to a foreign interest, three things happen. We have one fewer asset, and we have one asset more in foreign exchange of the same value. Then counterpart funds are created against the foreign exchange to pay the farmer. The result is that we have one asset less, one asset more, and one liability more, all being of the same value. We are poorer by the value of the sale.

This same problem appears when we export more in value than we import. The asset which is exported for a foreign exchange asset, causes a money supply increase to pay the exporter. Until the foreign exchange is used to bring in an import, reversing the process, we are the poorer for it.

The term "a favourable balance of trade" is often used to describe a situation where we export more than we import. This is a nonsense as we are poorer in this circumstance. A national balance sheet will evidence, demonstrate, and measure this.

This Comprehensive Balance Sheet offers a good deal of reassurance to Australians. With our total net assets at $19,108.4 billion, and our population of 25.69 million, our net assets per each are $743,806.92. That is nearly $3 million per family of four.

Somewhere there must be a reason why Government doesn't bother to tell us this good news.

Compiled and presented by Charles Pinwill

A NATIONAL SUPPLY AND DEMAND ACCOUNT

(PROFIT AND LOSS ACCOUNT) FOR THE COMMONWEALTH OF AUSTRALIA IN THE YEAR ENDED 30 JUNE 2020

Section A – Aggregate Personal Income available for Consumption

Item	Notes	SAUD Billions
Wages and Salaries	P&L 1	798.1
Personal Dividend Income	P&L 2	37.9
Personal Interest Income (monetary received only)	P&L 3	32.7
Social Security and Insurance	P&L 4	161.4
Less Individual Income tax paid	P&L 5	-235.9
Less State and Local Government Fees and Charges and other Commonwealth taxes on individuals	P&L 6	-156.8
Proprietor's Income	P&L 7	160.8
Household Debt Servicing Payments	P&L 8	-67.8
Superannuation and Life Insurance receipts in cash less direct personal contributions	P&L 9	65.1
Total Aggregate Personal Income available for Consumption		**795.5**

Section B – Gross Consumer Production

	Notes	SAUD Billions
Personal consumption component of GDP (actual)	P&L 10	1047.5
Net Consumer Goods Imported (food, beverages, automotive products and other items) less exports of same = 100.4 less 65.1	P&L 11	35.3
Gross Consumer Production available for purchase		**1082.8**
Deficit of consumer purchasing power in the year to 30th June 2020		**287.3**

NOTES

<u>P&L 1</u>. The ABS figure for Wages and Salaries of $953.9 billion (ABS Table 36, Line 71, as adjusted in March 2022) includes secondary income deemed to be part of wages and salaries. Superannuation contributions from employers are included, although these will not be available to consumers for decades. From the ABS Table 36, total Social Benefits and Assistance paid by employers, though not quantifying superannuation, and including the Medicare Levy, is given as $145.9 billion. In addition to this, Workers' Compensation of $9.9 billion which is paid by employers is deemed to be wage payments. These two figures totalling $155.8 billion must be deducted from wages proper. Actual wages and salaries paid directly to employees therefore are $798.1 billion.

P&L 2 and 3. ABS Table 36 gives personal income from dividends and interest as $38.4 and $32.7 billion respectively. It also gives a figure for the reinvestment of these as $0.5 billion. As reinvested income is not available as purchasing power for consumption this amount has been deducted from dividends to reflect this.

P&L 4. Itemised from ABS Table 36: Workers' Compensation $9.8 B, Non-life insurance net claims over premiums ($48.4 minus $42.7) to equal $5.7 B, and Social Benefits (or social security) of $145.9 to total $161.4 billion.

P&L 5. The ABS Table 36 gives income tax paid by individuals as $235.9 billion.

P&L 6. The url https://alga.asn.au/facts-and-figures/ from the Australian Local Government Association gives Local Government rates collected as $18.9 billion in 2018-19.

The url https://www.abs.gov.au/statistics/economy/government/taxation-revenue-australia/latest-release gives total taxation in Australia in 2020 as $552.0 billion.

It also gives Company Income Tax as "down $7.1 billion which is minus 7.5%." Therefore the size of this tax is ($7.1 billion divided by 7.5 and X by 100) and equals $94.6 billion.

GST is given as down $1.1 billion or 1.7%. Its size is therefore $1.1 billion divided by 1.7 and X by 100 and so GST was $64.7 billion.

This account measures income available against consumer goods and services offering. Direct tax impacts by reducing income, and indirect taxes such as GST by increasing prices. As GST is reflected in increasing the value of consumer production available, it is not also deducted from income.

Other taxes paid by individuals therefore equals $552.0 billion, less individual income tax already given in the account of $235.9 billion, less Company tax of $94.6 billion, and GST of $64.7 billion

P&L 7. ABS Table 36, line 71.

P&L 8. The ABS Table 36, under Secondary Income Payable (other current taxes) gives interest paid on Dwellings and Consumer Debt as $52.8 and $6.5 billions respectively. Interest paid on Unincorporated Enterprises and rent on Natural Assets are given as $7.5 and $1.0 billions respectively. As these detracted from personal purchasing power in the year to 30th June 2020, the total given is minus $67.8 billion

A deduction for principal repaid in the year upon previous consumption should also be made here, as it is not available for present consumption. This figure is, however, unavailable.

P&L 9. The purpose of this item is to determine the impact of superannuation upon personal purchasing power. This requires the discovery of the amount of superannuation payouts, and a figure for individual contributions into superannuation.

The rate of employer contributions into superannuation was 9.5% of wages which is, from P&L 1, $798.1 billion. Employer contributions were therefore $75.8 billion.

In the ABS Table 29, Superannuation is not differentiated from Life Insurance, as is the case throughout the ABS statistical offerings. Total contributions into super and life insurance is given as $169.8 billion. By deducting the employer contribution of $75.8 billion going into superannuation we arrive at a figure of $94 billion for individual contributions into them.

Claims against both superannuation funds and life insurance are given as $159.1 billion. Net receipts to persons were therefore $159.1 minus $94 billion, or $65.1 billion.

It should be noted here that this was an unusual period with the Covid pandemic causing heightened superannuation withdrawals, and an unusual increase in these funds flowing to individuals.

<u>P&L 10 and 11</u>   This data was confirmed in an email from Dom Williams [mailto:dom.williams@abs.gov.au] on the 31st of March 2021 giving the links https://www.abs.gov.au/statistics/econ omy/national-accounts/australian-system-national-accounts/latest-release and also https://www.abs.gov.au/statistics/economy/international-trade/bal ance-payments-and-international-investment-position-australia/latest-release

What this Account Means

The fact that consumer products produced by the Australian people were $287.3 billion more that were the inducements to produce it by way of incomes distributed, has enormous significance. If a company paid its employees $X to produce, and the value produced was $X+Y, its profit would equal $Y. If all the profit were distributed as a dividend, then the dividend per share would be Y divided by the number of shares.

Since there were 25.69 million Australians in 2020, the surplus of consumer production over their available incomes to purchase it of $287.3 billion, amounted to $11,183.33 for every person, or to $44,733 per family of four.

Whilst it seems to be an impossibility that this situation could be survived, this is managed by the increase of Australian indebtedness. We must borrow to buy our profit, because while we have it in goods, we don't have it in cash. Australian indebtedness has increased every year since federation in 1901, and when its increase is insufficient, we go into recession.

By visiting the "Debt Clock" at http://australiandebtclock.com.au/ its "necessary" continual increase may be observed. At some point on the 4th March 2022 Total Government Debt was $1,476 billion and Total Private Debt was $5,175 billion for $6,651 billion in all. Dividing this by the population gives every person's share (adults and children too) of the debt as $249,194.

If governments regularly did this type of Profit and Loss Accounts for their nations, the practice of financing the necessary consumption increases by increasing indebtedness to the banking system may be reconsidered. It is, at least theoretically, possible to create and issue money debt free when extra funds are necessary to augment consumption.

Accounts such as this raise the question of what it might mean in terms of public policy.

The Purpose and Utility of this Account

The purpose of this account is to measure the income available to the Australian people in a period (2020), against the consumer goods available in that same period. This provides the most accurate indication as to whether an increase in credit is needed to facilitate the full consumption of desirable goods and services. Further, it quantifies this need and helps to establish a credit policy which neither causes demand pull inflation nor a recession in the economy.

For this reason, it offers an important guide to policy makers in determining the optimum increase, or in extremely rare occasions decrease, in the money supply and credit made available.

No official account of this type has been done in Australia up to 2022. This being so, the statistics of the Australian Bureau of Statistics are not always constructed in a way most useful to producing this account. This often compels, necessarily, extrapolation and assumption which brings statistical approximation. No apology is made for these limitations to the account's accuracy; quite the contrary, really, as these demonstrate and evidence the need for "custom made" data suited to our purpose.

Juxtaposing the aggregate consumer goods produced and available, against the inducement paid to produce them in the form of incomes, while it measures supply in the form of goods and effective demand which is incomes, allows the account to be properly seen as a National Profit and Loss Account constructed from the point of view of Australia's people, who, properly considered, are the nation's shareholders, all holding one share each at par value.

When the decision was made to do the first ever National Profit and Loss Account, it was for the United States in the year 2014. At the outset the concepts and principles to be employed were set forth. They are reproduced here to assist in conceptualising the accounts intent.

Principles Adopted in the Preparation of this Account

1. The purpose of production is consumption.

2. The cost of production is consumption (that is, the consumption appertaining to it).

3. The purpose of a national economy is the objective good of its people (i.e. to deliver the goods and services that they need to survive and flourish, while calling upon the least amount of labour and resource consumption). This excludes employment, corporate profits or economic growth per se as the end social objects.

4. Calculations of Gross Domestic Production are measures of human *activity*, not of results or outcomes from this activity considered in terms of human satisfaction.

5. That National Supply and Demand Accounts, (the commercial equivalents of which are Profit and Loss Accounts), though nowhere in existence, when constructed from the perspective of accessing the economic satisfaction of its national proper persons, are the best measure of a Nation's economic performance. Just as company accounts are done from the perspective of shareholders, this account is from the perspective of a Nation's people, not its management or clients.

6. This account has been constructed with a view to ascertaining aggregate personal income available to enable personal access to the gross national consumer production available.

7. While all GDP ($17,393.1 billion in the US in 2014) is ultimately

paid for by consumers, either in prices or taxes, capital goods have been removed from this account as their inclusion in prices, usually as depreciation charges, does not take place until a later period of time.

8. GDP treats exports as increased production activity, while this account treats exports as a decrease in production availability.

9. It was resolved, as a principle, to proceed in spite of analytical difficulty. National accounts as currently available, while no doubt approximately accurate for their intended purpose, are careless in differentiating proper person's receipts, for example, from "private" receipts. As a result the GDP component "Personal Interest Income" is given as $1,300.9 billion, while "Personal Interest Payments" are $254.2 billion and Mortgage Interest Payments are $387.0 billion for a total of $641.2 billion. This implies a clearly inaccurate situation where proper persons have loaned out over twice the sum of their debts. Thankfully this conundrum was resolved by accessing http://www.bea.gov/iTable/iTableHtml.cfm?reqid=9&step=3&isuri=1&903=288 which enabled *imputed interest* which is now present in current interest income to be expunged. Imputed interest is not purchasing power available to consumers until a later period of time.

10. Notwithstanding the dearth of clear data specific to proper persons, and differentiating them from private corporations in many items, this account was persisted with, not because of its likelihood of achieving *accuracy* but because of its absence, and in the hope of advancing the realisation that the true measure of an economy's performance in terms of human outcomes (see 3 above) is calculable (and probably only calculable) along the approximate lines used here. This Account can at least provide a template which, with refinement and correction, and perhaps one day specifically Government generated data to its purpose, will be able to more accurately inform us.

Input with this intent would be most welcome.

Those wishing to access the full 2014 Profit and Loss Account for the United Stated in 2014 can do so at http://www.socialcredit.com.au/uploads/NationalAccountsPrototype.pdf

It is exceedingly strange that Governments do not make every effort to share the good news that our economies are profitable beyond $11,000 each, which surely, we would all be happy to know.

Compiled and presented by Charles Pinwill

PART SIX

THE FRUITS OFFERING FROM UNDERSTANDING

CREDIT: THE MEANS TO SUPER-HEGEMONY

H egemony is attained when one State, entity, people, or sanction gains predominant influence and decisive superior power over others. The classic example is the hegemony won by Imperial Rome over all other peoples and political competitors in the Mediterranean by means of its Legions.

It was a decisive hegemony indeed, which lasted for centuries. It was not, however, a super-hegemony. While Rome certainly had military and political hegemony, social hegemony over the human organism eluded it. It had no sufficient means at hand to influence what the people thought, or thought about, and in time it was conquered by the Christian faith, though the continuing disharmony of aspirations and ambitions brought incursions from neighbouring peoples and the dissolution of the imperial administration.

The ownership of land as the means of sustaining human life in medieval Europe then became the key sanction, though its exercise was at most provincial and decentralised, with little extenuated influence.

The monopoly of land faded as the mobility of products brought in the mercantile system with the re-emergence of increased trade via waterways and re-established roads.

Trade demanded a currency, and while commodities such as honey and salt served for a time, these were progressively displaced by credit. This was largely done through "letters of credit" issued by the banking families of northern Italy, such as the Medici, whereby claims for value were exchanged and accepted with commercial entities at the mouth of the Rhine and other important centres of trade. Money in the form of credit had arrived.

In time, practically all trade was reconned and organised through a money system of bank issued credit to be settled at some future time. Credit was also issued by wealthy merchants and trading houses whose substance and credit-worthiness were trusted, though as time progressed the business of providing credit was almost wholly swept up into the emerging banking houses.

Through this, banking evolved into more highly organised forms. The establishment of the Bank of England in 1694 was a key development. Together with other commercial banks all credit was issued, created and given out with security, to serve as society's money and our system of the claims of each against the other.

Credit at its creation was costless. Once a claim to redeem it was made, it could only be met by acquiring a bank deposit owned by another. Thus, buying and selling were wholly performed with bank deposits which were entirely created without cost, initially, through the function of banks making loans, which became the deposits of their payees.

Modern money is created and issued as loans of credit by banks, though ownership of that money is always retained by these banks via a mortgage over the assets of the borrower. Modern societies have, in net terms, no money at all. Their medium of exchange is always the debts of others, and society considered as a whole, only has the money which it owes to the banking system.

Here is the super-hegemony of credit which is increasingly evident and all-pervasive. Wall Street has long taken America in hand. Even their Federal Reserve Bank is privately owned through a system of regional banks, though their ultimate private owners have never been disclosed.

America's debt is approximately $90 trillion, and though some of this is owned by those who have obtained the bank deposits of others and reloaned, ultimately it is all the property of the private banking system. They not only own the $90 trillion, but through their power to costlessly issue credit, they have also come to own all that money will buy where their interests suggest advantage and they determine to buy it. Imperium has made many suggestions.

Human beings have both strengths and weaknesses, and sometimes both are contained in the one attribute. An example of this is our inclination to cooperate, to comply with majority opinion whenever we can, to support consensus and common ideas and objectives. This is supportive of social harmony. Historically, it has enabled enormous progress toward the achievement of objectives delivering benefits in terms of human satisfaction.

Time was when ours was an organic culture. All of the people in a community, both those of the present and the past, had contributed to our cultural heritage in some way. Some may have contributed a useful phrase, helped in finding a productive process, given us a recipe, a concept in thought, an observation of the truth, and each in his way gave something to our economic, cultural, or spiritual inheritance. This inheritance is now so enormously significant that it contributes more to our wellbeing than can individual effort alone.

This very progress enabled the instruments of artificial consensual culture to be established. It began with the printing press and grew with radio and television. The whole of the mass media was available for purchase with money and is now bought and paid for.

Our cooperative instinct is such that we find it very difficult to believe anything other than what most people apparently believe. This reached a point where Richard Nixon was able to say that the American people will never believe anything that they have not seen on television, and it was difficult to disagree.

We are very vulnerable to accepting what we are most often told, and suspicious of contrary notions and the consequences of dissent. If the media never tells us that the banks create and own all of our credit, exact a rent for it, and are ambitious of even a global hegemony, this challenges credulity and our natural inclination towards social harmony.

Other key influences over thought also fell prey to the power of creating credit. One of these was in education.

Universities and educational institutions of all sorts are dependent upon - and therefore vulnerable to - grants, bequests, endowments, scholarships, and other forms of financial support. These are best had by not offending the donors thereof. Teaching truths prejudicial to the interests of those most able to contribute is a "heavily felt hand". Major tax-free foundations progressively took up the burden of educational research, and this too carried a bias beneficial to the "Golden Internationale", if the interdependent and collaborative consortium of international credit-creating houses can be properly so called.

In time this Golden Internationale recognised and identified its contending forces and institutions, and increasingly focused its attention towards undoing their influence.

At the point of its ultimate end, which is probably some type of global hegemony, where peoples are children responding to the benevolent administrations of an empowered and kindly elite, the end of an ungoverned sanction to create and own the people's credit will likely arrive. The definitive end of the human organism will be accomplished, and all the future determined.

This future will probably not be scary and infinitely evil in the Tolkienian conception, but it will continuingly reside in the power of the one ring: the means of privately creating all the claims which we hold one against the other, which is now euphemistically called "credit".

The overwhelming majority who hold the human organism in their hearts as beautiful, must somehow come to the minority view that it is vulnerable, and that it is exposed to capture by the monopolisation of credit.

The issue of all new money creations on the basis that we all participate in our common inheritance and prosperity, and that it might be a dividend bequeathed to us as a legacy of our forebears, will, if it can be acted upon, undo our enslavement.

The West's peoples are oblivious to ideas of a golden internationale pursuing global hegemony. It could not be otherwise, as it has never been explained on television. The above exposition is no academic speculation, notwithstanding its limited recognition. In the world of well organised high-powered intelligence organisations it stands in central position, and is brightly lit. This burst into the open in 2017.

In that year in Munich, President Putin, in the presence of many high-ranking American officials, made a speech in which he made it emphatically clear that Russia would not cooperate in the building of a "Unipolar World".

When the Soviet Union dissolved in the 1990s it was envisioned that it would gradually be enmeshed and entangled in myriad financial arrangements which would render its economy inseparable from the financial umbrella which is cast over Europe, America, Japan and elsewhere. The oligarchs, with Western finance, quickly swept up the major industries in Russia such as oil and aluminium.

Then Putin interrupted the process. Some of the oligarchs were exiled, some jailed and their property confiscated. Russia would not cooperate in a programme to govern the world from one point; Russia would be opposed to the unipolar world.

From this point onwards the undoing of Putin was prioritised. NATO broke its treaty obligations and moved its armed forces up to the Russian borders. Sanctions were imposed on Russia. The CIA assisted Zelenskyy into office in the Ukraine with an anti-Russian policy. Provocation and response from both sides will take years to play out and may flare into a more serious conflict at any point.

The contest between the programme of a credit-creating elite with global ambitions and the rest of us, can only end in one of two ways. Global hegemony may be attained and maintained with whatever severity proves sufficient, or alternately, money supply increases, when needed, may be distributed to us equally as a dividend on the basis of our industrial inheritance.

This ring of power will not be destroyed in the cauldron of a volcano, but rather, by casting it into the arms of us all.

AFTER DARKNESS

I t is entirely possible, human presuppositions notwithstanding, that vast expanses of truth-knowledge may never occur to a single human mind and remain forever in a dominion of unvisited darkness. Pride in our intellectual prowess resists denial of the ultimate omnipotence of our knowledge, for knowing what we don't know is forever an arena too far. Approach it as we may, there is always an indistinguishable and indiscernible something beyond.

What comes after darkness, is only a light upon our former ignorance. For this reason, knowledge can only ever teach us humility: the ultimate enlightenment about the human condition and our only guide into the future.

While to the prideful this is a philosophy of despair, to the devotees of truth it brings an exhilarating humility in the contemplation of the fullness of the grandeur of the full glory of reality. In knowing that reality transcends human thinking we become its apprentices and begin to learn. We don't learn *everything*, but we do learn *more*.

There are plenty of examples. By the fifteenth century the Chinese had long concluded that they knew everything and had stopped their former considerable efforts to explore the rest of the world. When the Portuguese came in their wooden ships, commandeered their seas and their foreign trade, they saw it as humiliating. Once enabling humility was commanded, they could again grow and learn, accept their shortcomings, and thus re-establish nationhood.

Preconceptions about the flatness of earth, the sun's daily circumnavigation of the earth, and scurvy being the result of vapours, amongst countless other misconceptions, once abounded.

Misconceptions, though notable and numerous, are only part of it. Non-conceptions are equally extraordinary. In all the writings of the ancients, from Mesopotamia, China, Egypt, Greece and Rome there is no discoverable text suggesting that the chattel slavery of human beings was not OK. The first mild suggestion that slavery might be put aside from human relationships came from St. Paul around 60 AD (the Epistle of Philemon).

St. Paul had been influenced by his Lord who never made a statement against slavery. He didn't have to. His idea that all had value in the sight of God and had innate value to a God who loved them, left the obvious to unfold in time. In only 1800 years black slavery in America, and a little later white slavery of Europeans in North Africa, was ended.

Yes, it is certainly humiliating. That the idea that slavery was not the way of just relationships took 7,000 years from first civilisation to occur to anyone and a further 1800 years to become established policy, must bring a measure of hesitancy to our intellectual pride.

Since such is possible, our confidence that we now know it all is somewhat tenuous is it not? Could it not be that a like darkness in other areas of human social arrangements may persist even now?

I am not here going to attempt a large exposition of one of the large darknesses of modern society of which I have been privileged to acquire some knowledge. It involves the coming of an alternate slave-master, the hegemony of the debt mastery over society.

Counterfeiters don't really exist any more. No nations' annual budgets itemise revenue from any money creation, yet all created out of nothing in cyberspace, it certainly now is. Money creation is now the business of central banks in association with private banks. Although the need for it results from the whole efforts of the community, its ownership is not shared.

Our only access to money is by borrowing it from these creators (they never give it away) and they only ever rent it to society with a rental charge which is called "interest". Therefore, if we own a little money, it has all come from some borrower and he must return it. We pay for it, if borrowed by industry in increased prices, and if by government in taxes. If we borrow it as consumers, we must pay by reducing later consumption.

When our incomes from producing are insufficient to buy the resulting consumer goods, more debt is added to the already high world indebtedness which has now burgeoned to beyond $200 trillion, globally.

The credit creation mechanism which properly began in the West after the establishment in 1694 of the Bank of England, grew until it displaced chattel slavery as no longer being necessary to the wholesale control of persons economically. A means of creating and sharing our "money votes" in a way similar to which we create and distribute our "ballot paper votes" is explored in other of my essays.

This essay is to explore a world after which this form of population control has also been conquered.

In this new world about 20% of our incomes would come from the needed money supply increases being shared equally. The earliest measurement of this profit of society to be shared can be found at http://www.socialcred-it.com.au/uploads/NationalAccountsPrototype.pdf It shows that this would have brought payments to each American in 2014 of $7,500, or $30,000 per family of four. A more recent National Account for Australia in 2020 shows it bringing over $11,000 to each Australian or approximately $44,000 per family.

The financial stress levels in society would be immeasurably lessened. We'd no longer be wholly dependent upon being employed, or upon taxation and social security giving us the employment revenue of others. We would not be driven towards debt, and then stressed by the need to find its repayment. A more relaxed society in which we have more time for each other would be a most joyful result.

With debt atrophying it would bring a somewhat different world. It has often been observed in the animal kingdom, that scarcity is the preconditioning causation of greed. When food is plentiful there are no violent contests for it.

Men are so motivated. Plenty to the point of sufficiency is an essential harbinger to peace on earth, and goodwill towards men.

A cultural flowering of music, harmonious communities, literature, sport and the contemplation of all forms of beauty and fellowship, are easily envisaged in this world. We need to make a little time now to imagine how it can be. I will not prompt these imaginings further just now; it is best performed as a do-it-yourself activity.

Curiously, when asked "Who are you?" most will say "I'm butcher... baker... farmer... candlestick maker". We think of ourselves, apparently, as something like minions in a termite nest; I'm a worker, I'm a drone, I'm a soldier. I once witnessed a fellow being asked who he was and he responded, "I am a male Caucasian heterosexual homo sapiens who loves wine, women and song." A bystander then said "Well that puts you into a minority, doesn't it" and thereupon the whole party fell into laughter. How strange that someone would think other of himself, than as an economic functionary!

It is much more useful, accurate and true to categorise people in terms of what they love, surely? He's a family man, a football fan, a Church goer or some breed of political animal perhaps. While all slaves love their chains, as ours fall away with harvested energy and applied technology displacing us, we will begin to think of ourselves rather more as humans, and rather less as functionaries. Who shall we then say that we are?

It is altogether possible that in a world of regularly paid national dividends, we may enjoy enough leisure to discover what this is. So, if you are actively doing something, how do you know whether it is work or leisure? There is only one sure test. Did someone else tell you to do it and offer reward, or did you decide to do it for yourself? In the former case it is work and, in the latter, leisure. The contention that leisure is laziness, indolence and unproductive is the product of those who fear that we will increasingly govern our own actions, but this will dissipate with increasing National Dividends regularly paid to all.

One of the plagues which will cease to torment us is advertising. Because all businesses must now compete for your scarce purchasing power to survive, this advertising plague may be likened to one of flies on a hot day. You have only to open your eyes to have them flying into them from every direction. Billboards, signage, and invasive television and YouTube assaults are everywhere we look. Advertisements assault our mouths and our noses at every opportunity for a culinary presentation. They assail our ears with every noise which can be made to exist to stop us thinking our own thoughts, and contemplate their dreary and dreadful merchandise.

We don't mind people telling us what they have to offer in a civil and low-key manner, but to be constantly attacked with every means of prompting consumerism by appealing to us to increase our social standing, prestige, attractiveness to the opposite sex, or ability to attract attention is beyond what we might be expected to endure. Urging consumerism invades and inhibits our most precious asset, the time and peace in which to think our own thoughts without interminable promptings.

Those who have been increasingly freed from financial stress and the clutter distracting us into a false sense that happiness emanates from consumerism, will be better equipped to discover a powerful key towards contented happiness. What is that?

Building your "toolbox" to enhance your ability to enjoy a self-examined life is a key here. We live our lives and find our happiness within. The world and all within it, are just the background of life, not its substance. The water of life comes from an inner spring, not an external flood.

A post "credit-slavery" world's benefits will be found within the personal centre of each of us. We are going to have to win what of this we can, to enable us to give birth to a culture beyond debt slavery. This is the work of the 21st Century. It has begun. You have just been recruited. Relax, be tolerant with yourself and don't expect miracles until your toolbox of the means of understanding it has been more fully furnished.

Your long journey has already begun if you have taken a first step.

Epilogue

Achieving DMC

If we are going to explain, advocate, and eventually achieve DMC, thousands of people will need to become involved in supporting it.

This will require us to associate together in advancing DMC towards its implementation in society. To begin this, a website https://www.democraticm oneycreation.com has been established. It answers frequently asked questions and provides useful resources such as videos and written articles and books. In time, it will grow in these services.

Most importantly, however, the website offers a forum in which all may participate simply by logging in with Facebook, a Google account or any email account. You may then join in the discussion at any existing posts or create a new post, and you will receive notifications of any new activity. A community which helps its members to grow in understanding, provides promotional ideas and materials, and in time, maybe even organises events.

The most critical thing beyond all else in attaining DMC will be personal initiative. A centralised structure which directs us will not happen and should not. The one thing which is beyond suppression and external control is well considered personal initiative. If DMC's supporters can generate and display abundant personal initiative this will command the future.

Starting from even modest beginnings, by associating together, a people's movement for DMC will be able to grow throughout the social media, the natural leadership of the movement will emerge, multiple internet forums may be established, and DMC will gain an international following.

Be of good cheer, for there is no force on earth as powerful as *a good idea whose time has come.*

Yours faithfully,

Charles Pinwill, Author

ABOUT THE AUTHOR

C harles Pinwill was born in 1945 to pioneering farmers, and had a happy
rural childhood in Gayndah, Queensland's oldest town. An early childhood experience – an overheard conversation between adults speculating that
the directive control of the world was in very few hands - proved pivotal, igniting
an enduring fascination for the challenge of returning the jurisdiction of money
to its legitimate owners, the general public. After local primary schools he
attended an academic secondary school, Brisbane Grammar, before returning
home to farming. He was active in the Junior Farmer/Rural Youth organisation,
serving on its State Council for several years and participating in its debating
competitions.

In 1969 with his brother Don he bought *Yaramulla,* nearly 70 square miles of
fertile undeveloped land in North Queensland, developed it as a cattle station,
and later grew potatoes and other crops. They did all the development and stock
work themselves, including water drilling. In the early 1980s this property was
requisitioned by the State Government as a National Park, and subsequently has
produced absolutely nothing at all. The property contained the Undara Crater
and many lava tunnels which the brothers were the first to explore.

In the 1970s Charles actively campaigned against the imposition of Death
Duties and contributed to this tax's abolition throughout Australia. An avid

reader, he has since his youth preferred the areas of history, politics, and finance-economics.

His previous publications include *Democratising Money* and *Democratising Banking,* and an earlier work of essays called *Different Essays (They're Certainly Different).*

Charles is married with three grown daughters.

Nowadays he describes himself as a very unfit, ornery and cranky old man. Furthermore, he claims his feet stink, his dog won't bite, and he doesn't like peanut butter sandwiches.

WHERE TO BUY AND MORE TITLES

This book is available by visiting www.democraticmoneycreation.com and clicking on the "Books Available" heading.

Other titles by Charles Pinwill:

Different Essays (They're Certainly Different)
Balboa Press 2021

Democratising Banking
Freedom's Booksearch 1995

www.ingramcontent.com/pod-product-compliance
Lightning Source LLC
Chambersburg PA
CBHW032135020426
42334CB00016B/1168